DR LIVINGSTONE, I PRESUME?

DR LIVINGSTONE, I PRESUME?

MISSIONARIES, JOURNALISTS,
EXPLORERS, AND EMPIRE

CLARE PETTITT

Harvard University Press
Cambridge, Massachusetts
2007

First published in Great Britain by
Profile Books Ltd,
58A Hatton Garden
London EC IN 8LX

Library of Congress Cataloging-in-Publication Data
Pettitt, Claire.
Dr. Livingstone, I presume? : missionaries, journalists, explorers, and empire / Clare Pettitt.
p. cm.
Includes bibliographical references and index.
ISBN-13: 978-0-674-02487-8 (alk. paper)
ISBN-10: 0-674-02487-7 (alk. paper)
1. Livingstone, David, 1813–1873. 2. Stanley, Henry M. (Henry Morton), 1841–1904.
3. Explorers—Africa, Sub-Saharan–Biography. 4. Explorers–Scotland–Biography.
5. Africa, Sub-Saharan–Discovery and exploration. 6. Africa, Sub-Saharan–In mass
media. 7. Africa, Sub-Saharan–Colonial influence. 8. Great Britain–Relations–United
States. 9. United States–Relations–Great Britain 10. Great Britain–Foreign relations–
1837–1901. 11. United States–Foreign relations–1865–1898. I. Title.

DT1110.L58P48 2007
916.704´20922–dc22   2007016390

For my 'Good Doctor',
Dr Luke Hughes-Davies,
and everyone at the Oncology Unit,
Addenbrookes Hospital, Cambridge –
thank you

CONTENTS

Maps   viii

Introduction   1
1   Livingstone   13
2   The meeting   71
3   'Faithful to the end'   124
4   Stanley   179

Further Reading   211
List of Illustrations   225
Acknowledgements   228
Index   232

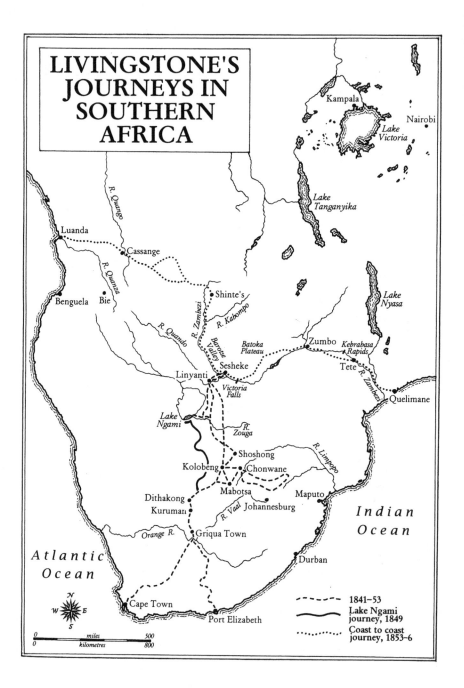

LIVINGSTONE'S JOURNEYS IN SOUTHERN AFRICA

Kampala

Nairobi

Lake Victoria

Lake Tanganyika

Luanda

Cassange

R. Quango

R. Quanza

Benguela Bie

Shinte's

Lake Nyasa

R. Kabompo

R. Quando *R. Zambezi*

Baroise Valley

Batoka Plateau

Zumbo *Kebrabasa Rapids*

Linyanti Sesheke

Tete *R. Zambezi*

Victoria Falls

Quelimane

Lake Ngami

R. Zouga

Shoshong

R. Limpopo

Kolobeng Chonwane

Dithakong Mabotsa Maputo

Kuruman *R. Vaal* Johannesburg

Indian Ocean

Orange R. Griqua Town

Atlantic Ocean

Durban

N W E S

Cape Town

Port Elizabeth

| 0 | miles | 500 |
| 0 | kilometres | 800 |

– – – – 1841–53

——— Lake Ngami journey, 1849

··········· Coast to coast journey, 1853–6

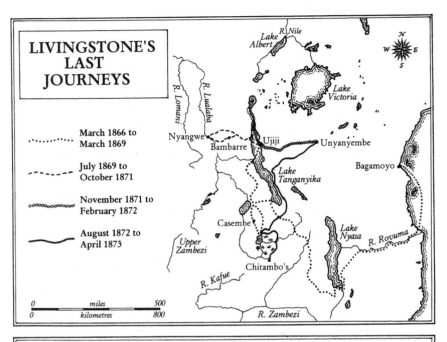

LIVINGSTONE'S LAST JOURNEYS

········· March 1866 to March 1869

– – – July 1869 to October 1871

ooooooooooo November 1871 to February 1872

～～～ August 1872 to April 1873

R. Lomani
R. Lualaba
R. Nile
Lake Albert
Lake Victoria
Nyangwe
Bambarre
Ujiji
Unyanyembe
Bagamoyo
Lake Tanganyika
Casembe
Lake Nyasa
R. Rovuma
Upper Zambezi
Chitambo's
R. Kafue
R. Zambezi

0 miles 500
0 kilometres 800

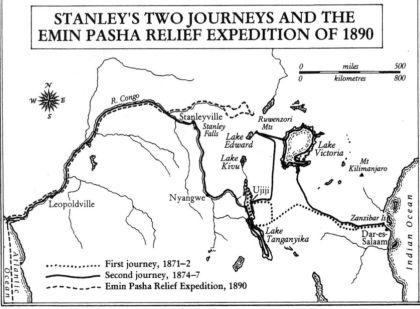

STANLEY'S TWO JOURNEYS AND THE EMIN PASHA RELIEF EXPEDITION OF 1890

0 miles 500
0 kilometres 800

R. Congo
Stanleyville
Stanley Falls
Ruwenzori Mts
Lake Edward
Lake Kivu
Lake Victoria
Mt Kilimanjaro
Nyangwe
Ujiji
Leopoldville
Lake Tanganyika
Zanzibar Is
Dar-es-Salaam
Atlantic Ocean
Indian Ocean

············ First journey, 1871–2
———— Second journey, 1874–7
– – – – Emin Pasha Relief Expedition, 1890

'Memory, so far from being merely a passive receptacle or storage system, an image bank of the past, is rather an active, shaping force; that it is dynamic – what it contrives symptomatically to forget is as important as what it remembers – and that it is dialectically related to historical thought, rather than being some kind of negative other to it.'

Raphael Samuel, *Theatres of Memory* (1994)

INTRODUCTION

A is for Africa – unknown and wild
B is for Blantyre – where he lived as a child
C is for Cape Town – he landed there first
D is for Desert – the country of thirst
E is for Elephant – tusks good for trade
F is for Forest – he marched unafraid
G is for Gospel – he lived and he taught
H is for Healing – that sick people sought
I is for Illness – yet he would not despair
J is for the Journal – he wrote up with care
K is for Kuruman – home of Mary his wife
L is for Lion – nearly lost him his life
M is for Makololo – he led safe and sound
N is for Ngami – the first lake he found
O is for Ox – that he rode on the track
P is for Patience – when things look black
Q is for Quilimane – an African port
R is for Rapids – in which he was caught
S is for Slaves – he strove to set free
T is for Tent – a poor shelter you see
U is for Ujiji – where Stanley came
V is for Victoria Falls – he gave them their name
W is for Wainwright – of the last faithful band
X is for 'Ex'ploration – to open the land
Y is for You! – 'Carry on' as he said
Z is for Zanzibar – where they brought him when dead.

Published in 1941, a hundred years after Dr David Livingstone sailed from London for Africa, the garishly illustrated *Alphabetical Adventures of Livingstone in Africa for Boys and Girls* summed up his life for a wartime generation of British children. All the major components of the myth that developed around Livingstone are here – his exploration of Africa, his campaign against slavery, his medical training and his Christian faith.

And, crucially, Stanley. Although Stanley is only given a walk-on part in these *Alphabetical Adventures*, Livingstone would never have been so universally remembered had Henry Morton Stanley not donned his pith helmet and gone to find him. It is the meeting between the newspaper reporter from America, Stanley, and the Scottish missionary-explorer, Livingstone, in Ujiji, in what is now Tanzania in East Africa, in October or November 1871 that is best remembered today. Almost everyone knows Stanley's famous greeting to Livingstone, 'Dr Livingstone, I presume?' No word had been heard from Livingstone since 1869 and Stanley went out to Africa while working for the American newspaper, the *New York Herald*, to find him, when the British were still getting a relief party together. 'It was one of the most famous meetings in history,' the 1960 British Ladybird book *David Livingstone* confidently tells its child readers. And indeed it is. It is recycled over and over again – an episode of the television soap *ER* is called 'Dr Carter, I Presume?', an episode of *Star Trek* is called 'Dr Bashir, I Presume?', and so on. But why have Livingstone and Stanley become so obstinately embedded in both British and American culture?

'At primary school I do not remember being taught any "facts" about Livingstone beyond the encounter with Stanley and the pilgrimage of the African porters,' remembers one

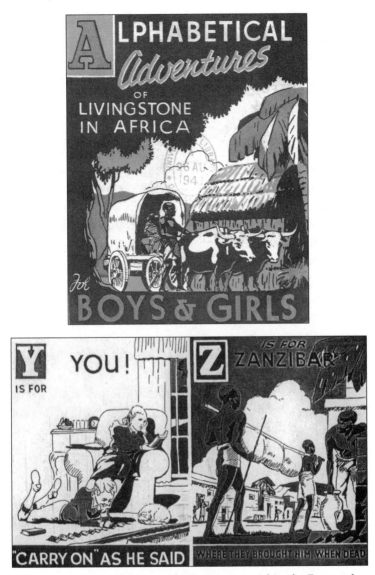

1. Alphabetical Adventures of Livingstone in Africa for Boys and
Girls: *a wartime pamphlet published in 1941.*

historian. The story of the meeting has been told and retold, although few people know about Livingstone's faithful black servants, who carried his body back to the coast after his death. In 1928, *David Livingstone: Heroic Missionary, Intrepid Explorer and the Black Man's Friend*, another book written for children, described the meeting:

> As Stanley crossed the last ridge of the mountains and saw the little port by Ujiji below him embowered in palm trees, he gave his excited men the signal, and volley after volley from nearly fifty guns broke the silence of the lake. Three hundred yards farther and they met natives streaming out in hundreds to look at them.
>
> Stanley pushed through the crowd and saw a semi-circle of Arabs, in front of whom was a white man with a grey beard. He was pale, and looked old and wearied, and had on a consul's cap with a bit of faded gold lace round it, and a red-sleeved waistcoat and grey tweed trousers.
>
> 'Dr Livingstone I presume?'

By the time Stanley emerged from the jungle and 'found' him, Livingstone had spent most of his adult life in Africa. He had gone out as a Protestant missionary in his twenties, but – much to the disgruntlement of his employers – he did not settle in one place, as most missionaries did. Instead, he had made several celebrated journeys across Africa, from coast to coast, and up the Zambezi river. His vivid accounts of his explorations quickly established themselves as best-sellers in Britain and America, as the public – who had no idea what might be in Africa – were amazed and delighted by the descriptions of verdant fertile plains, lakes and abundant wildlife in his 1857 *Missionary Travels*.

Livingstone was fêted when he returned to Britain between 1856 and 1858, but rather than staying at home to enjoy his celebrity he went back to Africa, because he was becoming increasingly obsessed with locating the source of the Nile – the holy grail of Victorian geography. Things did not go well, however. His Zambezi expedition of 1858–64 ended in failure and was recalled by the British government, and the Universities' Mission, which was Livingstone's idea and was set up around the same time to send graduates as missionaries to Africa, was nothing short of disastrous. Many Europeans died and Livingstone was to some degree responsible for their deaths. In 1866 *The Times* sadly declared, '[W]e cannot refrain from censuring the man whose rash counsels led these sheep to perish in the wilderness.' But public interest in Livingstone was rekindled when, at the end of 1866, an account of the explorer's death – false, as it turned out – was received in Britain. It had been sent on 10 December 1866 from Dr G. E. Seward, the Acting Political Resident at Zanzibar, to Lord Stanley, Secretary of State for Foreign Affairs. Edward Daniel Young, who had been with Livingstone on the Zambezi expedition, offered to arrange an expedition for the Royal Geographical Society (RGS) to investigate the truth of this report. The Society instructed him to bring back something 'tangible – something known to have belonged to Livingstone, which he would not have been likely to have parted with voluntarily', thus underlining the difficulties of proving the authenticity of travellers' reports in this period. Young later recounted how he had followed a trail of clues that established Livingstone to be alive and on the move, although he never actually caught up with him: 'An empty cartridge case (Enfield) was brought to us, and an iron spoon of English make with the word "patent" upon it.' He was also shown a little English prayer book, a small looking glass and an English-made razor. These cheap and banal objects shone out to Young as evidence of a British presence. The matter was clinched when he questioned a black African about a white man who had passed through the village – Young asked what he had been wearing on his head and was told, '[a] covering which was black and a piece of something in front (here he imitated the peak of a naval cap most admirably, by holding his hands over his forehead)'. Young returned to England, reporting Livingstone to be alive. Later, he would be criticised by the *New York Herald*: '[I]t is not very apparent why they did not proceed on their errand in any case. From their own statement it was because of their own certainty that Livingstone had been found to a sufficient extent and did not desire to be found much more.'

Livingstone was indeed still alive, but things were getting increasingly difficult for him. Illness and slave-trade-related disturbances forced him back to Ujiji, an Arab trading town on the eastern shores of Lake Tanganyika. In July 1869 he set out again with a friend, one of the Arab traders, Bogharib, for Manyema, west of Tanganyika, hoping to reach the River Lualaba and follow it north. In Manyema he was knocked out by fever, anal bleeding and – the worst of all – deep ulcers on his feet that meant he could not walk for months. The British Consul, John Kirk, back in the consulate in Zanzibar, did manage to get supplies as far as Manyema. Livingstone was stuck at a town called Bambarre from July 1870 to February 1871. Eventually, he got up and going again, and by the end of March he was at the town of Nyangwe, but he needed to cross the Lualaba and the Arabs refused to help him or lend him canoes, as they were

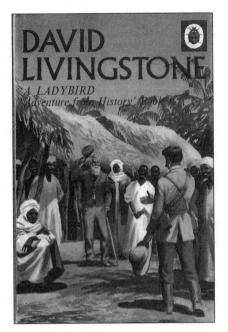

2. *The cover of the 1960 Ladybird children's book which kept the story alive for the baby-boomer generation.*

suspicious that he might be spying on their slaving activities. On 15 July 1871 Livingstone witnessed a massacre of the African inhabitants of Nyangwe by the slavers. When the shooting started, terrified people rushed into the river, where hundreds drowned. Livingstone was running out of paper, but he kept writing on any scraps he could find, determined that this atrocity should be recorded. 'As I write I hear the loud wails on the left bank over those who are there slain, ignorant of their many friends who are now in the depths of the Lualaba. Oh, let Thy kingdom come!' he prayed. Afterwards, the Arabs admitted to 400 dead – most probably an underestimate. Livingstone was horrified and now felt he could never accept Arab help again. He realised he was stranded. His medicine chest had been lost in 1867, which he saw as 'a sentence of death by fever', his instruments were damaged and the British government seemed to have forgotten about him. There was nothing for it but to return to Ujiji, where he had left supplies in 1869. But when he arrived on 23 October 1871, he discovered that his £600 worth of goods had been sold or stolen. This was very bad news. Slaving-related violence meant it was unlikely that Kirk would be able to get anything through from Zanzibar for months, '[b]ut to wait in beggary was what I never contemplated, and now I felt miserable'. In fact it would be only a matter of days before Stanley arrived to utter his famous line and to relieve Livingstone.

Back in Britain no news had been received from Livingstone since the appearance of a letter dated 30 May 1869 and many presumed that this time he really must be dead. Eventually a British relief party, which included Livingstone's youngest son, Oswell, was again organised by the RGS. But they were too late. Their expedition had only just left Zanzibar when it encountered the returning Stanley, who had already found Livingstone, been on an exploration of his own with the doctor around the lake, and then left him with generous supplies and a new party of men, and was now triumphantly carrying Livingstone's 'huge Letts's Diary', letters and geographical reports back to Britain.

The winner of the race to find Livingstone, Henry Morton Stanley, had been born into poverty in North Wales, grown up in a workhouse and emigrated as a teenager to America, working as a shopboy in a store serving planters in the American South to earn a living until the American Civil

War, when he fought on both sides and afterwards became a war reporter. He was employed by the enterprising American newspaper editor James Gordon Bennett Jr, one of a new generation of newspapermen who saw that news could be created as well as merely reported. In his best-selling book *How I Found Livingstone* (1872), Stanley made much of Bennett's summons to his Paris hotel room and his instruction to an amazed Stanley to 'FIND LIVINGSTONE'. But actually, Bennett seems to have told him to do a grand journalistic tour of the Middle East rather than to find Livingstone. He sent Stanley to cover the opening of the Suez Canal, then up the Nile to write a tourist guide, on to visit Jerusalem, Constantinople, the Crimea, the Caspian Sea, Persepolis (where Stanley would sleep in the ruins and carve his initials on a temple pillar), the Euphrates and India. This represented about a year's worth of travel, reporting on ruins and other non-time-sensitive stories before even starting for Africa. Reports of Livingstone were mixed – some said he had been eaten by cannibals, others said he was still living. It seems that Livingstone was not high on Bennett's news agenda at all, and that it was probably largely Stanley's decision, rather than his employer's, to risk the trip into Africa on very uncertain information in the hope of producing a scoop. 'I was too far from the telegraph to notify you of such expense or to receive further orders from you,' he later explained to Bennett. It is unclear what Stanley would have done had Bennett refused to pay the bills for $8,000 that he had racked up by then.

Stanley's triumph created an enormous sensation in the newspapers in Britain and America – throughout the summer of 1872 they were full of the story of the meeting. From the material in Livingstone's papers carried back from Africa by Stanley, the British press gave particular prominence to Livingstone's graphic exposures of the horrors of the slave trade, including the powerful account of the Nyangwe massacre which precipitated a fundamental change in British policy: '[T]he movement of the legislature is held to be due to the frightful revelations made by Dr Livingstone,' reported the *Illustrated London News*. The slave market in Zanzibar was shut down by the British in June 1873. In America, Livingstone's celebrity was more closely tied to Stanley and to the American triumph in 'rescuing' him. But on both sides of the Atlantic, Livingstone was once again immensely famous – as his friend Horace Waller wrote to him that year, 'mention of your name makes the rafters shake!'

But Livingstone was never to receive Waller's letter. By June 1873 he was indeed dead. He had refused to come back to Britain with Stanley and had stayed on to try once more to establish the true source of the Nile. He became so ill that he had to be carried along by his servants on a stretcher, and finally they built him a hut to lie in. Here he died in Chitambo's village in May 1873. What followed was remarkable. His black African servants, organised by two of their number – Abdullah Susi and James Chuma – decided that Livingstone's body should be returned to his people. His heart and other internal organs were buried in a 'tin box, which had formerly contained flour' under a tree in the village, but the rest of his body was dried out in the sun and wrapped in calico, then covered in tar and disguised to look like a bale of cloth. They risked their lives carrying Livingstone's body the thousand miles and more to the coast, where it was shipped back to Britain aboard the *Malwa*. The black African Jacob Wainwright, who had entered Livingstone's service only in August 1872, accompanied the coffin to England. His passage was paid for by the Church Missionary Society (CMS), but nobody offered to pay for Susi and Chuma to travel to England. They were brought over later by Livingstone's friend James Young, who had made a fortune out of paraffin, but they missed Livingstone's elaborate funeral. The *Malwa* arrived at Southampton docks on 15 April 1874 'amid a general manifestation of public feeling as remarkable as it was impressive'. Livingstone's mummified body was interred in Westminster Abbey on 18 April 1874. Stanley was a coffin-bearer. 'All ranks, from the very highest to the humblest in the land, vied in paying him honour,' reported *The Times*. Livingstone's enduring fame as a manly Christian missionary who fought against the Arab slave trade in Africa was firmly established.

Yet the truth was more complicated. Livingstone had often cooperated with the Arab traders; indeed, they had often kept him alive with their supplies, and he had fallen back on their kindness at Ujiji when Stanley found him. Livingstone's missionary activities had been a failure: he made only one convert in Africa, who subsequently lapsed. The two missions he led to Africa were misconceived and badly planned, and resulted in the miserable deaths of more than half of the missionaries and their families. As an explorer he had had more success, but what his mourners did not know in 1874 was that his most impressive geographical achievement – the discovery of the source of the Nile – was in fact a misidentification.

Without Stanley and the famous meeting, we would probably not remember Livingstone. And without Livingstone, Stanley would never have achieved such enduring fame. But there is more here than meets the eye. The story lodged so firmly in the Anglo-American consciousness for reasons

that were not just to do with these two extraordinary individuals. This was the first sensational news story to break
simultaneously on both sides of the Atlantic. The Atlantic
cable which made this possible had gone down only a few
years before and this was the first eruption of a kind of global
media celebrity with which we are only too familiar today.
The handshake between the two men was also politically
timely: it was a fitting symbol of a thaw in Anglo-American
relations after all the bitter feeling over the American Civil
War. Despite a position of official neutrality, Britain had
materially supported the Confederacy of Southern (slave-
holding) States and the victorious North had demanded
financial reparation for this after the war. These claims were
settled just as Stanley's rescue of Livingstone hit the news
in the summer of 1872. It was perfect: Stanley's report of
Livingstone's fierce anti-slavery agenda would not only
bolster the Union in the States, but also, more importantly,
help to wipe out memories of Britain's support for the South
in the Civil War, re-establishing an Anglo-American alliance
based on the 'new' values of the American Union – values of
democracy and freedom. So the story's immense resonance
in the nineteenth century, which has kept it current to this
day, was intimately tied up with an important shift in Anglo-
American culture in the 1870s. Moreover, what looks like a
simple story actually has relevance to some of the biggest
and most complex issues which still affect us today: technology and its transformation of social relations; the growth of
celebrity culture; and the tricky issues that remain around
the relationship between America and Britain.

1

LIVINGSTONE

As soon as Stanley's description of the meeting hit the news in Britain and America in the summer of 1872, 'Dr Livingstone, I presume?' became instantly famous as a phrase and was immediately appropriated by music-hall comics, popular songwriters and advertising copywriters. By the end of 1872, *Fraser's* magazine was able to dismiss 'Mr Stanley's story [as] so well known' that it was not worth the retelling, and even in September, only a month after Stanley's scoop had hit the front pages, the episode of the meeting was familiar enough for Mark Twain to be able to parody it on his visit to Britain, making a speech in which he claimed to have got there first, and recalling that '[Livingstone] had nothing to wear except his venerable and honorable naval suit, and nothing to eat but his diary. But I said to him: "It is all right; I have discovered you, and Stanley will be here by the four-o'clock train and will discover you officially, and then we will turn to and have a reg'lar good time."'

Throughout the 1870s, Stanley's line was endlessly parodied in Britain and America. In the States, Palmer Cox, the popular illustrator and writer, and creator of the 'Brownies', published *That Stanley!* in 1878. Less good-natured than Twain's version, this is a long poem in mock heroic couplets which tells of Stanley's search for Livingstone, but the really

3. A rare photograph of Livingstone aged 51 taken in 1864 by Thomas Annan on the explorer's last visit to Britain.

dark comedy is in the illustrations. Bennett, for example, is seen peeping out at the end of each canto, interested only in 'the profits of his enterprise' as

> soon on railroad-car or boat,
> In cities near, and towns remote,
> The *Herald* fluttered, thick as leaves
> When Autumn for her foliage grieves.

Many of the jokes are scurrilous, as when Stanley on his journey through Africa comes upon a black African woman with a white baby:

> Here sat a dame the hue of night,
> Whose son and heir was partly white;
> And there a child, black as a crow,
> Surprised him with a head of tow.

When he discovers

> A missionary man devout,
> That Brooklyn city had sent out.
> 'Ha! Ha!' quoth Stanley, 'here my friends
> At last the infant problem ends.'

The joke is doubly wicked, because the reader has been led into thinking that the father of these mixed-race children may turn out to be Livingstone himself. Stanley's alleged cruelty to black Africans is graphically illustrated as he tortures them for information about the whereabouts of Livingstone:

> At times he'd threaten one with death,
> And even stop awhile his breath.

The comedy of Palmer Cox's long joke poem rests upon the already tiresome fame of the Stanley and Livingstone story, which nobody has been allowed to ignore:

> The lisping infant has been taught
> How Stanley found the man he sought;
> And age with failing eye has scanned
> The pages from our hero's hand.

So it seems that the very fame of the story at the time generated more and more ironic retellings, and created a momentum that has kept it spinning along right into the twenty-first century.

Indeed, the Stanley and Livingstone story remained most visible in the twentieth century through comedy. In 1930 the Marx Brothers' first film was released. The precarious and haphazard plot of *Animal Crackers* revolves around the return of the celebrated Captain Spaulding (Groucho Marx) from Africa, and certainly owes much to both Stanley and Livingstone, and possibly also to Twain. Jack Benny performed a parody of Stanley's search for Livingstone on his 1940 radio show, making his Stanley character practise the phrase 'Dr Livingstone, I presume?' over and over again on his way to find the missionary. Artie Shaw and the Gramercy Five recorded 'Dr Livingstone, I Presume?' in 1940 too. The 1949 MGM musical *On the Town*, starring Gene Kelly and Frank Sinatra, includes a scene in which the character Brunhilde Esterhazy quips, 'Dr Kinsey, I presume?' – a very topical reference the year after Alfred C. Kinsey's book *Sexual*

4. *Palmer Cox's 1878 illustrated poem* That Stanley! *made fun of Stanley's immense popularity in the States and the enormous readership of his bestselling* How I Found Livingstone.

Behavior in the Human Male was published. Indeed, when the book first came out, a newspaper cartoon depicted a man squinting through the keyhole of a hotel-room door and being accosted with the words, 'Dr Kinsey, I presume?' The central character in Abbott and Costello's 1949 film *Africa Screams* is called Stanley Livington. In 1968 the sexual revolution that Kinsey had helped to kick-start was under way and the British band the Moody Blues released a song called 'Dr Livingston [*sic*], I Presume?', which recruited Livingstone the adventurer and explorer into the psychedelic mindquest of the late 1960s. And in 1983 a version of Livingstone returned for a whole new generation. Jim Henson created a muppet of Dr Livingstone for the American cult children's television show *Sesame Street*. In the sketch, Bert and Ernie are searching for Dr Livingstone in the jungle and they know there is some important phrase they must remember to say when they find him. When they reach him, Ernie blurts out, 'What's up, Doc?'

The most famous contemporary image of the meeting between Stanley and Livingstone was a double-page engraving which appeared in the *Illustrated London News* on 10 August 1872. Our attention is naturally focused upon the two central figures – the muscular, bearded individual doffing his pith helmet to the older, frailer-looking man, in worn, sagging clothing, who in response raises his battered peaked cap. Stanley certified that this image was 'as correct as if the scene has been photographed'. But on closer inspection, it contains some less familiar aspects. What did contemporary readers make of the conspicuous presence of the Stars and Stripes flag behind Stanley? Or the men holding spears behind Livingstone, who seem to be not black Africans but Arabs? Or the many buildings in the background of the scene that seem to denote a large residential settlement rather than a clearing in the jungle? These details lead us straight into the symbolic complexity of this meeting but tend to drop out of the story in the memory, leaving just the central figures, alone in an African wilderness. They are, indeed, frequently literally dropped from later representations of the meeting, which is often shown taking place in a jungle clearing. But what actually happened at Ujiji in 1871? Why Livingstone went to Africa in the first place and what he did when he got there have slipped our minds. And quite why Stanley went out to find him is shrouded in mystery for most people too.

LIVINGSTONE IN THE NINETEENTH CENTURY

The spotlight of international celebrity fell on Livingstone on precisely three different occasions during the nineteenth century: once in November 1857, with the publication of *Missionary Travels* in England and America; again in

5. *Stanley meeting Livingstone as depicted in the* Illustrated London
News, *10 August 1872. Stanley certified that this picture was 'as correct as
if the scene has been photographed' although it is curious that the flags are
unfurling in a strong wind which does not seem to be blowing anything else.*

August 1872, after the meeting with Stanley; and once more
(although he had already been dead for a year) in April 1874.
Timing and technology had a lot to do with his name becoming known in every household across Britain and beyond.

But who was 'the Good Doctor'? As an adult, Livingstone
named a settlement in the Shire Highlands of Africa Blantyre
(now the capital city of Malawi). But when Livingstone was
born there in 1813, Blantyre was a small village on the banks
of the Clyde, about eight miles south-east of Glasgow, which
had been almost entirely built by the mill owners Messrs
Henry Monteith & Co. for the workers in their mill and
dyeworks, which were powered by the river. Livingstone's
family lived in a tiny tenement in the mill buildings and as
a child he was put to work in the mill as a 'piecer' – piecing

together the threads of cotton that broke during the spinning process – and later as a spinner. Livingstone's first book, *Missionary Travels*, includes some autobiographical material, but the story he gives of his childhood fits so perfectly the conventional narrative of the child auto-didact that one wonders how much he was, consciously or unconsciously, constructing himself in this way by then. For example, he tells us implausibly, 'With part of my first week's wages I purchased Ruddiman's "Rudiments of Latin".' While it is true that he was an ambitious child, and he was undoubtedly exceptional, it is also worth remembering that both his brothers ended up far from Blantyre too – one in Canada and one in North America – and that this pattern of emigration was not unusual in the period, particularly in Scotland. As John MacKenzie notes, 'Scots emigration was always proportionally higher than English', to the extent that one nineteenth-century traveller remarked, 'I began to think that either the world was very small or Scotland very large.'

Indeed, one of the most crucial things – perhaps *the* most crucial – to remember about Livingstone's identity is that he was definitely Scottish and not English. He spoke with a strong Scottish accent, at university he was educated in the Scottish tradition of science rather than classics, and because he was rarely to return to Britain during adulthood, the Scotland of the 1830s and 1840s remained as if preserved in aspic in his mind. *Missionary Travels* opens with quotations from the Scottish literary canon and not the English, from Walter Scott's *Lord of the Isles* and then Robert Burns's 'The Cottar's Saturday Night' rather than Shakespeare, or Greek or Latin literature, despite the fact that Livingstone did teach himself to read Virgil and Horace. In particular, the Scottish landscape of his childhood stayed imaginatively present to Livingstone throughout his African journeys. When he noticed little piles of sticks by the wayside in Africa, for example, he remarked upon how they were stacked up 'cairn fashion'. And in his *Missionary Travels*, it seems that almost every river he encounters in Africa is compared, somewhat improbably, to the Clyde: 'Coming down the river Zouga we now had time to look at its banks. These are very beautiful, resembling closely many parts of the river Clyde above Glasgow.'

Livingstone grew up in the strict and unforgiving Scottish Calvinist tradition of election and predestination. It was only when he was a teenager that his father became a Congregationalist and adopted a more liberal theology that allowed the possibility of salvation for all. The Congregationalists in Scotland had strong links with Congregationalists in the United States, so meeting Stanley was far from Livingstone's first encounter with America. He read a lot of American theology and American liberalism became a very important strand of his thinking while he was still in his teens. Through his chapel, he was well informed about the Atlantic slave trade a long time before he was to see its horrendous practices in action. Stanley later remembered Livingstone being able to recite the American anti-slavery poets 'Longfellow, Whittier, and Lowell' by heart. British anti-slavery campaigners, known as Abolitionists, were very vocal in the 1820s, when Livingstone was growing up, and the pressure they put on the government resulted in 1833 in the abolition of all slavery in the British empire. Livingstone was twenty in 1833 and optimistic about the possibility of eliminating all such brutality from the world.

His Christian liberalism, though, was combined with an innate conservatism. He claims in *Missionary Travels* that ordinary people 'hate those stupid revolutions which might sweep away time-honoured institutions, dear alike to rich and poor'. In this sense Livingstone was, and remained throughout his life, oddly anti-progressive, with a respect for custom and tradition that was, perhaps, more influential on his relatively liberal approach to African culture than his involvement in more politically liberal campaigns such as that against slavery. At the same time, his medical training and his respect for science pulled him forwards into the future. Like Lydgate in George Eliot's *Middlemarch*, he was one of the first doctors to use a stethoscope, and, as a student, he had to explain to his puzzled examiners how this preposterous instrument was intended to be used.

While still working in the mill, he began to prepare himself for action and – amazingly – in the four years between 1836 and 1840 he was to transform himself from a factory spinner to a professional missionary-doctor setting sail for Africa. He paid with his factory wages to train part-time in medicine at Glasgow and then he won a place on the prestigious professional missionary course in theology at a London Missionary Society (LMS) seminary at Chipping Ongar in Essex. Livingstone set sail for Cape Town from London on 8 December 1840, leaving the metropolis at about the same time as a pregnant London maidservant, Elisabeth Parry, fled back to her father's cottage in Denbigh, North Wales, to give birth in January 1841 to an illegitimate child, before returning to her job without her baby son. Thirty years later that baby – John Rowlands – would meet David Livingstone in a remote town in Africa. But by then he would have changed his name to Henry Morton Stanley.

FIRST JOURNEYS: KURUMAN, MABOTSA AND THE BAKWAIN,
AND AFRICA COAST TO COAST

From Cape Town, Livingstone journeyed by ox wagon to a
mission station in Kuruman, in the northern Cape in South
Africa. Kuruman was run by the Scottish missionary Robert
Moffat, whom Livingstone had met in London earlier that
year, and who had become something of a hero for the
younger man. Livingstone loved the travelling in Africa.
'The mere animal pleasure of travelling in a wild unexplored
country is very great,' he wrote, and he describes his journeys as 'a prolonged system of picknicking, excellent for the
health, and agreeable to those who are not over fastidious
about trifles, and who delight in being in the open air'. He
would never have agreed with Stanley, who, impatient with
the slow pace of African travel, wished for a railway in order
to catch up with Livingstone faster. Livingstone loved to walk
and was ambivalent about the technologies that went with
his ideal of commerce and civilisation for Africa. In a wonderfully self-contradicting remark, he describes the African
scene before him: 'Hundreds of buffaloes and zebras grazed
on the open spaces, and there stood the lordly elephants
feeding majestically, nothing moving apparently but the
proboscis. I wished I had been able to take a photograph of
the scene, so seldom beheld, and which is destined, as guns
increase, to pass away from earth.' He does not seem to have
fully comprehended the link between the camera and the
gun, or have realised that his own memorialising impulse to
landscape painting and word-pictures in *Missionary Travels*
went hand in hand with his stated aim to 'open up' Africa:
'My desire is to open a path to this district, that civilization,
commerce and Christianity might find their way there.'

He was to find the missionary work here more difficult

than he had imagined, however. The view of missionary work given back in England by the LMS and other fund-raising bodies was an idealised one. Livingstone and others had been brought up with scenes of the whole population of African villages gratefully accepting the Christian message as one after drinking in an inspirational missionary sermon. The famous evangelical, Charles Spurgeon, was to perpetuate this myth, preaching to twelve thousand people in London in 1859, he declared 'Mr Moffat and our great friend Dr Livingstone have been labouring in Africa with great success, and many have been converted.' This misconception persisted well into the twentieth century: the 1939 Twentieth-Century Fox film, *Stanley and Livingstone*, includes a ludicrous scene in which Stanley is woken the morning after he has found Livingstone at Ujiji by the sound of singing – the whole village is giving a joyful rendition of the hymn 'Onward Christian Soldiers' with enthusiastic tambourine accompaniment, conducted by Livingstone himself. As Arthur Sullivan's famous music for this hymn was not written until December 1874, the use of it in this scene is anachronistic as well as absurd. The real Livingstone discovered, when he tried preaching to them, that the villagers were more likely to stand on their heads, 'burst ... into uncontrollable laughter', or take fright and hide under any available bench. The African tribes they encountered often welcomed missionaries, but not for the word of God, so much as for their engineering skills, their beads for trading and their medical knowledge.

Livingstone had been wondering how on earth he would ever find a wife in Africa and now he was presented with Mary, one of the Moffats' two daughters. Mary Moffat and David Livingstone were married on 2 January 1845. After

6. *Livingstone conducts African villagers in a rousing rendition of 'Onward Christian Soldiers' in the 1939 American film,* Stanley and Livingstone.

Kuruman, Livingstone founded his own station at Mabotsa, and then moved again to live with Sechele's people – he was chief of the Bakwain (now known as the Kwena) – at Chonuane, where he and his new wife were based from 1846 to 1851. Livingstone's biographers have never given him much credit as a romantic lover, and it is true that the letters that survive to his wife are significantly less engaged and informative than those to his male friends and, latterly, to Agnes, his grown-up daughter. Much has been made of Livingstone's description of his new wife as 'a stout stumpy body'. Certainly, his subsequent treatment of Mary was not always tender. He impregnated her constantly (whenever they spent any time together, it was inevitable that Mary would discover shortly afterwards that she was pregnant). He considered African contraceptive practices

– particularly the sexual abstinence sometimes insisted upon for three years after a child was born, or before the menfolk went into the jungle on long hunting trips – to be 'absurd'. In fact, many western couples in the Victorian period also used abstinence as a way of planning their families. Not so David Livingstone, though, who fathered five children within six years, and impregnated Mary again in 1858, the only other time they spent together. Having got her pregnant, he joked about her as 'the Irish Manufactory' (conventional racism against the Irish portrayed them as breeding too much), as if it were all her doing, and then dragged her across African deserts – as his mother-in-law furiously pointed out – with no thought for propriety: 'A pregnant woman with three little children trailing about with a company of the other sex, through the wilds of Africa, among savage men and beasts!' she exclaimed in a letter to Livingstone.

Indeed, a case has been made for Mary herself as a pioneer African explorer like Mary Kingsley. She certainly walked and wagoned her way across as much if not more of Africa than any other European woman in the nineteenth century, and Livingstone saw nothing peculiar at all in this, and does not seem ever to have considered her feminine modesty. 'Your Mama was famous for roughing it in the bush and was never a trouble,' he wrote to his daughter Agnes, after Mary's death.

At the end of the 1851–2 journey from Kolobeng to the Cape, where Mary and the children were to set sail for Britain, it was not Livingstone but William Cotton Oswell, an English gentleman who had met Livingstone while big-game hunting in Africa and subsequently funded some of his African explorations, who kindly went ahead to buy 'a

7. *The illustration in Murray's 1857* Missionary Travels *of Livingstone's mauling by a lion 'larger than a hippopotamus'.*

very necessary outfit for Mrs Livingstone and her children, their garments having by time and travel been reduced to such rags – albeit well-mended – as to be hardly fit for their appearance in Cape Town, much less for the proposed voyage home'.

But it was Livingstone, and not his wife, who was to be celebrated for his heroism. The story of Livingstone's mauling by a lion in 1844, which left him with a broken arm, early became an important part of the heroic iconography around him. Indeed, with some embarrassment he objected to his publisher, John Murray, that the illustration of this incident in *Missionary Travels* was 'absolutely abominable ... it really must hurt the book to make a lion look larger than a hippopotamus'. In fact, Livingstone's heroism is debatable in this, as in many other matters. He was saved from death by others, having approached the lion foolishly 'with only one gun and no armed native at his side'. One of his servants, Mebalwe, snatched a gun from another native and fired, missed, but distracted the lion, which turned instead on Mebalwe, who sustained a serious wound on his thigh, while another African who joined the fray was badly bitten on the shoulder. Livingstone was indubitably badly injured by the lion – as he records, 'Besides crunching the bone into splinters, he left eleven teeth wounds on the upper part of my arm' – and he had to set his own shattered bone, which must have been excruciatingly painful, but Mebalwe and the other man suffered too. Furthermore, all three men could have avoided injury completely had Livingstone not 'very imprudently', as he later admitted, decided to attack a lion who had just killed some sheep and was likely to defend its kill if interrupted. Often, in Africa, Livingstone's acts of solitary heroism turn out to be acts of impetuosity and inexperience (as in this case), from which he was usually extricated by Africans who understood their own country, and its flora and its fauna, much better than he could. Nevertheless, several casts of Livingstone's arm – or his left humerus, to be exact – have been preserved as sacred and heroic relics. The British Royal College of Surgeons has one. In April 2004, a bronze sculpture of Livingstone being attacked by an enormous lion was presented to the David Livingstone Centre in Blantyre, Scotland, by the Hollywood special effects animator Ray Harryhausen, celebrated for his work on films such as *Jason and the Argonauts* and *Clash of the Titans*. Harryhausen said that he had designed the six-ton statue because he 'wanted to bring heroes back into fashion. Heroes are inspirational figures and David Livingstone was certainly one of those.'

It is arguable, in fact, that many of Livingstone's 'heroic' characteristics – his near-obsessive drive and an optimism that degenerated into self-deceit – eventually drove his long-suffering wife to alcoholic despair, and his firstborn son to desperation and an early death in the American Civil War. When his own children were small, he cruelly exposed them to terrible risks – including six days in the desert travelling without water until they could not walk and their tongues turned black from dehydration, and one of his baby daughters died at a month old after his wife had endured another such journey by bumpy wagon in the last stages of pregnancy. These were his first serious explorations in Africa in 1849 and 1850 – journeys to Lake Ngami. Barbara Kingsolver read *Thirty Years' Adventures and Discoveries of Dr David Livingstone and the Herald–Stanley Expedition (1872)* while she was writing her best-selling 1998 novel, *The Poisonwood Bible*. In the novel, the wife and four daughters of the evangelical Baptist Nathan Price tell the story of their father's disastrous attempt to establish an American mission in the Belgian Congo in 1959. The book is about the misprision between the Americans and the Congolese – a misprision that ends in tragedy and the death of the family's youngest child. Nathan Price clearly owes something to Livingstone in his stubbornness and his refusal to take his family home against all advice. Livingstone finally sent his family to Britain in 1852.

When Mary and the children arrived back, they led an unsettled life of borderline poverty, moving from one rooming house to another, thrown on the charity of the LMS as Livingstone's income – of £100 per year – was woefully insufficient to support such a large family and his own life in Africa. This never seemed to exercise him too much either. Financially, things did get better after the publication of *Missionary Travels* in 1857, and various government pensions followed, but Livingstone spent much of this money on philanthropic schemes in Africa, and his family never became rich as a result of his celebrity. At his death, the total value of Livingstone's estate was declared to be under £1,500. Mary undoubtedly felt abandoned by her husband and constantly sought to get back to Africa to rejoin him. Inevitably, though, the minute she did manage this – joining the Zambezi expedition in 1858 – she had to be sent more or less straight back to her parents at Kuruman because she had become pregnant and was suffering morning sickness. Livingstone did not hear of the birth of his daughter Anna Mary until more than eighteen months later. Anna had a very hazy idea of her father – she remembered him bringing her a black doll from Africa, and how she would have preferred a white one.

In 1853, now unencumbered by small children, Livingstone set off on his first great journey – walking coast to coast the 1,200 miles from Linyanti to Luanda. It was pretty miserable going – in extreme heat or torrential rain, with frequent stops as communities made demands for *hongo* (tolls or payment in cloth or beads as a price for crossing community territories) – and often downright dangerous. The majority of European travellers in Africa in this period died; Livingstone proved exceptionally tough. He was often helped during this ordeal by the Arab traders, who knew the terrain well. In fact, many of these traders were not really 'Arabs' but Muslim Africans enslaving other Africans. However, Livingstone always referred to the slavers indiscriminately as 'Arabs', perhaps as a way of mobilising British outrage against them.

Unlike Stanley, who carried – or rather made others carry – among other things, a turkey carpet, a hip bath and a bottle of champagne into the African interior, Livingstone travelled light, dismissing '"nicknacks" advertised as indispensable for travellers' and taking only a few objects with him, although 'not forgetting to carry my wits about me'. He took his medicine chest, a nautical almanac, Thomson's logarithm tables and a Bible. His most precious pieces of equipment were his sextant, made by Troughton & Sims of Fleet Street, a chronometer watch with a stop hand made by Dent's of the Strand, an artificial horizon and a pair of compasses. Despite this equipment, though, Livingstone's field data were not always scientifically accurate. On the coast-to-coast trip, for example, he tried to measure the breadth of a river with a piece of cord, but his men broke it by mistake. Nevertheless, it was while on this trip that Livingstone became convinced that on the Bakoka Plateau, miles from the coast, he had finally found his 'promised land' – non-malarial, fertile country, perfectly adapted for a mission.

LIVINGSTONE RETURNS TO BRITAIN, 1856–8; MISSIONARY TRAVELS (1857)

Having walked across Africa, coast to coast, Livingstone returned to Britain. Mary met him at Southampton docks on 12 December 1856, but she and the children would not see very much of him on this trip – he was far too busy being a national hero.

Honours were showered upon him. Just two days after he set foot on British soil again, he was presented with the RGS gold medal, and other ceremonies followed thick and fast – the freedom of six cities, honorary degrees at Oxford and Glasgow, an interview with the Prince Consort and an interview with the Queen. Two thousand guineas were raised for him by public subscription and he was nearly mobbed on Regent Street. He insisted on wearing his hallmark peaked 'consular' cap everywhere and clearly thoroughly enjoyed himself. Between January and July 1857 he wrote *Missionary Travels*. The LMS was running a £13,000 overdraft, and so it was very much in its interest for David Livingstone to be lionised as a great missionary too – and Livingstone did nothing to suggest that he was no longer involved in conventional missionary work. Privately, though, Arthur Tidman, Foreign Secretary of the LMS, sent Livingstone a letter saying the Society could no longer support him in plans 'connected only remotely with the spread of the Gospel'.

In November 1857 a handsome volume appeared from Murray's. Bound and cornered in dark green leather with wine-coloured, marbled board covers, it was quite expensive at a guinea (that is, just over £1, when the average annual income was £27 in 1857), although some booksellers offered it at a discount for 17s 6d. But this did not stop David Livingstone's account of his sixteen years' residence in Africa and his explorations, *Missionary Travels* – which was in fact more travels than missionary – becoming an instant and ubiquitous success. It sold more than 70,000 copies and made its author in excess of £12,000 – a fortune in the mid-nineteenth century. It had great popular appeal in Britain and the States. Indeed, *Missionary Travels* had been published simultaneously in America by Harper & Brothers. In 1875, they were selling a cloth-bound edition for $4.50, which was about the same price as the British edition. *Missionary Travels* was as well received in America as it was in Britain: 'It is a wonder-book all through,' enthused the *New York Courier and Enquirer*, for example. From 1857 Livingstone started to appear in cyclopedias and popular collections of biography in America, such as Chas B. Seymour's *Self-Made Men* of 1858. The popular periodical press began running articles on him too, often with portraits that could be cut out and pasted into scrapbooks or commonplace books, or displayed as pictures, such as that offered by the American monthly *Ladies' Repository* in June 1869. By the early 1870s, Stanley was confident that '[a]s many Americans had read [Livingstone's] books as Englishmen had done'.

Livingstone's British publisher, John Murray, a firm which specialised in travel and exploration books, and two years later would publish Charles Darwin's *On the Origin of Species*, had helped to create a keen public appetite for reading about exploration, adventure and natural history. Africa was of particular interest to this public because, as Edward Young remembers, it was still largely a blank on the map: 'that great white patch in Africa we remember in our school-boy days, and have pondered on as the well-thumbed Atlas lay before us; a burning desert – a second Sahara – was all that suggestion or wisdom could formally assign to it'. Here was a book that promised to reveal the secrets of that 'burning desert' in a conversational style that was accessible to all. For example, in *Missionary Travels*, Livingstone tells how he and his party came to the colossal waterfalls known by the local peoples as Mosi-oa-Tunya, or 'the smoke that thunders', which he immediately renamed the Victoria Falls. He describes the landscape in a vivid mix of poetic and scientific language:

> On the left side of the island we have a good view of the mass of water which causes one of the columns of vapour to ascend, as it leaps quite clear of the rock, and forms a thick unbroken fleece all the way to the bottom. Its whiteness gave the idea of snow, a sight I had not seen for many a day. As it broke into (if I may use the term)

pieces of water, all rushing on in the same direction, each gave off several rays of foam, exactly as bits of steel, when burned in oxygen gas, give off rays of sparks. The snow-white sheet seemed like myriads of small comets rushing on in one direction, each of which left behind its nucleus rays of foam.

Murray encouraged such lyricism in the writing and Livingstone added, 'scenes so lovely must have been gazed upon by angels in their flight', reinforcing an idea of Africa as a kind of Eden untouched by time since the Creation. Yet this accessibility caused Livingstone some problems. His scientific and geographical work was never taken entirely seriously by the RGS or the professional establishment, as is revealed by a discussion in the *Edinburgh Review*, one of the serious British quarterly journals, in a review of the five-volume *Travels and Discoveries in North and Central Africa* of Dr Henry Barth two years later in 1859. The *Edinburgh* was distinctly sniffy about Livingstone, the working-class Scot without a proper scientific training who got so much publicity, and commended Barth's work over the missionary's even 'though Livingstone has had the good fortune to obtain a higher degree of popularity from his personal adventures, from his missionary character, and from the daring character of some of his speculations'. But Livingstone's daring, unlike Barth's 'prolixity', sold books, and all over the western world people devoured his exciting account – Livingstone's mauling by a lion, his encounters with African communities and his outraged description of the slave trade in East Africa. The book brought cultural and colonial encounter right into British drawing rooms, just at the moment when another colonial encounter was exploding in the newspapers – the

Indian Mutiny, or Sepoy Rebellion, that had started in May and, through the newspapers, held the nation's attention to the end of the year. The horror that the British public evinced over the killing of British men, women and children in India gave a particular context to Livingstone's description of Africa as a land of pure potential, peopled by innocent 'tribes' – all poised for the advance of 'civilization, commerce and Christianity', in his own tripartite formula. Livingstone's descriptions of the regions that had been decimated by the slave trade – where he had seen human skeletons strewn on the ground in their hundreds – and his exhortations against 'this trade in hell' created a sensation too. Most people in Britain had thought that slavery was a thing of the past since it had been abolished across the British empire in 1833. Now they realised how wrong they were.

Missionary Travels is a curious amalgam of heroic adventure story, scientific observation, anthropological encounter, quest narrative and campaign literature, and it is liberally illustrated with engravings. Like the Americans, the British critics loved it. The Athenaeum got quite carried away, describing it as 'a book not so much of travel and adventure as, in its purport and spacious relation, a veritable poem'. Long extracts were published in the quarterly and monthly journals in Britain and America, ensuring that even those who did not read the whole thing read some bits of it. It reached the popular press too, which ran articles on the book and biographical features on Livingstone himself, immediately seeing his potential as a 'people's' hero. As far away as Krakow, Poland, a teenager named Józef Teodor Konrad Korzeniowski devoured the book and later claimed that it was Livingstone's Missionary Travels that had inspired him to become a steamboat captain on the Congo. As 'Joseph

Conrad', he would later publish one of the most ambivalent accounts of the Congo Free State, *Heart of Darkness* (1899).

Dubbed 'the Good Doctor', Livingstone was a hero who had pulled himself up by his bootstraps – a self-made man of the kind that Victorians particularly admired. Samuel Smiles, indeed, included him in his 1859 *Self-Help* and used a portrait of Livingstone as a frontispiece to later editions. Florence Nightingale compared him to John the Baptist, and George Eliot marvelled at how handsome he looked in his picture in *Missionary Travels*. Even Charles Dickens made him a heroic exception when he fulminated, 'Missionaries (Livingstone always excepted) are perfect nuisances, and leave every place worse than they found it.' In his own lifetime, even before he had met Stanley, Livingstone was a myth. He achieved that celebrity through the printed word – through his best-selling books and, later, through newspaper accounts of his exploits in Africa. Livingstone's story, then, is also the story of the growing influence of the press in the second half of the nineteenth century, and – as part and parcel of that – the emergence of a modern notion of celebrity. The whiff of disapproval that still rises from the pages of the *Edinburgh Review* reminds us that Livingstone's was a new kind of fame, and a kind that many in the establishment considered vulgar in its modernity.

Even in his lifetime, Livingstone's head, never without his 'consular' cap, was sculpted into umbrella handles and printed on boxes of matches. There was even a race-horse, Miss Livingstone, named after his daughter, which was racing regularly at Ascot and Newmarket in 1861. His portrait circulated widely, as either a cheap engraving or a more expensive photographic reprint. *Little England's Illustrated Newspaper* offered a portrait of Livingstone to its child readers in 1856, for example, for one penny, and in 1858 Livingstone was one of the 'Photographic Portraits' of 'LIVING CELEBRITIES' advertised for sale at 5s each in the newspapers. A part issue of *The Life & Explorations of Dr. Livingstone*, 'presented, Gratis, a Portrait of Dr Livingstone – size, 17 by 22 inches' with its first number.

On 4 and 5 December 1857 Livingstone gave two important lectures, one in the Senate House of the University of Cambridge, addressed to members of the university, and the other to the Mayor and Corporation of Cambridge in the Town Hall. The first lecture he pitched as a recruitment drive to the assembled students (all men at this time) and as such it was very successful, as many of those present were to become founders of the Universities' Mission to Central Africa. In these lectures, Livingstone made much capital out of the Indian Mutiny that year, and criticised the East India Company, suggesting that its tolerance of local customs and religions had led directly to the Mutiny: 'I consider that we made a great mistake, when we carried commerce into India, in being ashamed of our Christianity; as a matter of common sense and good policy, it is always better to appear in one's true character.' Livingstone suggested a new approach and the lectures show him to be rather more of a colonist than he was letting on to the government. Palmerston and the new Foreign Secretary, Lord Russell, were opposed to any colonisation plan that might alienate Britain's old allies the Portuguese, whose colony, Mozambique, already extended to the Batoka Plateau. 'These two pioneers of civilization – Christianity and commerce – should ever be inseparable,' Livingstone declared, and continued, 'Englishmen should be warned by the fruits of neglecting that principle as exemplified in the result of the management of Indian affairs. By trading with Africa, also, we should at length be independent of slave-labour, and thus discountenance practices so obnoxious to every Englishman.' Using an idea of noble and muscular English masculinity, he commended the life of the missionary to his audience of undergraduates: 'I would rather be a poor missionary than a poor curate,' he said. When he ended the lecture with the words, 'I LEAVE IT WITH YOU!' the applause and foot-stamping were ear-splitting.

The second lecture was aimed at an audience which was unlikely to produce missionaries but which Livingstone hoped to influence in favour of financially supporting his particular kind of missionary work. Consequently this was more of a trade-pitch, selling Africa as a kind of undiscovered cornucopia of untouched natural resources ready to drop into the laps of European investors:

> The people of that central part were anxious to have intercourse with white men, and their productions of indigo, &c. cannot fail to render commerce with them advantageous. Without the central basin, also, besides cotton, there are extensive coal-fields, with mine seams upon the surface, as well as an abundance of iron ore of the best quality. There is also produced a fibrous plant worth £50 or £60 a ton; and I have the authority of an English merchant to state, that a fabric finer and stronger than flax might be woven from it. The wild vine grows here in great abundance, and might be brought, by cultivation, to bear the most delicious grapes.

In both the lectures, Livingstone misrepresented the dangers and difficulties of the African terrain; he failed to mention his recurring fevers, his bowel problems, the frequent wars that made travel impossible for months at a time, and so on. As we shall see, his over-enthusiastic portrayal of Africa as a land of milk and honey was to have disastrous consequences for the Kololo mission and later for the Universities' Mission too.

THE ZAMBEZI EXPEDITION, 1858–64

In March 1858 Livingstone set off again for Africa on the British government-sponsored Zambezi Expedition. A year later, an LMS mission arrived at Linyanti at Livingstone's suggestion. It was to be a disaster. Two missionaries, Holloway Helmore and Roger Price, and their wives and children, joined the Kololo in February 1859, but the chief, Sekeletu, was insulted because Livingstone did not arrive with his family as he had promised. Livingstone had also promised to return the men he had borrowed from Sekeletu within a year; now four had passed and the men were still absent, and there were none of the promised traders coming down the river either. As a result of this disappointment, the Kololo, whom Livingstone had described as 'a jolly rollicking set of fellows', did not treat the missionaries well. Mrs Price became so thin she had to put plaster over her joints to stop the bones breaking the skin, and after she died and was buried some of the men exhumed her, cut off her head and presented it to Sekeletu. By Christmas 1859, six of the nine LMS mission group had died. Price and two of Helmore's children were the sole survivors. Livingstone's reaction when he was told of this disaster was appallingly cold-blooded. He showed no regret and blamed the missionaries themselves: 'a precious mull they made of it,' he wrote, showing the worst side of his character – an intolerance and refusal to confront or shoulder blame for anything which did not work out the way it was supposed to.

Meanwhile, the Zambezi Expedition was also in serious trouble. Livingstone had had to abandon the custom-built steamer, the *Ma Robert*, when it kept getting damaged on rocks and began to rust and leak hopelessly, and the expedition continued on foot. In the end only John Kirk went on with Livingstone, and on 2 December 1858 the two men were horrified to see the start of the Cabora Bassa Rapids. The irony was that Livingstone had been here before on his coast-to-coast journey and had completely missed the rapids because he had not realised the implications of the altitude measurements he had taken. Obviously, it would now be impossible to reach the Batoka Plateau by river. Livingstone's reaction to this disappointment was to do a swift U-turn: he switched all his attention to the River Shire instead. The Portuguese explorer Cardosa, whom he had met in 1856 at Tete, had told him that the Shire was fed by a vast lake. But Livingstone was soon to discover that the Arab Swahili slave trade had already reached the Upper Shire, and that fierce fighting was breaking out as Africans competed to cooperate with the Arabs. Unfortunately, Livingstone had already invited the Universities' Mission to the Shire Highlands. Almost as soon as they arrived, the missionaries were caught in the middle of a dangerous situation and Livingstone was forced to fire on Africans for the first time. In fact, the political situation in East Africa at this time was complex. Livingstone described the violence as 'tribal wars' but this is a nineteenth-century British interpretation of a historical and economically driven process in which the Yao were displacing the Manganga and other peoples in the region. When Bishop Mackenzie – the first Anglican bishop to reside in Central Africa – died of fever in January 1862, Livingstone began to get a bad press in Britain for not preparing the missionaries better. *The Times* felt that a 'heavy responsibility attaches to Dr Livingstone for the loss of these valuable lives'. Ultimately, four of the seven died.

Mary Livingstone arrived on the Zambezi again in 1862. Understandably enough, after five children and years of waiting for Livingstone to come home, she had become increasingly embittered and jaundiced in her view of missionaries and missions. Now she was cooped up with Livingstone in a tiny windowless cabin on the *Pioneer*. She offended the other missionaries on board by publicly criticising and ridiculing their work, and seemed to be almost constantly drunk, sometimes violently so. James Stewart had frequently to administer large doses of opium to her to keep her quiet at night. It was a sad and broken end for a woman who had managed the vicissitudes of her African and her British life with dignity for many years. Indeed, moving from the relative freedom of Africa, where she had run a school and organised her household minutely, right down to making her own soap, the transition to British conventions of 'gentility' and inactive 'ladylikeness' must have been difficult. Now she railed at Livingstone, blaming him bitterly for neglecting her and the children. She did have a point. Being the hero's wife had been distinctly less fun than being the hero. Livingstone was harried from all sides – his crew were also drinking excessively and raping local women, fathering children left, right and centre. In the midst of all this trouble, Mary Livingstone died of malaria at Shupanga on the banks of the Zambezi on 27 April 1862. She was buried under a baobab tree. Livingstone's grief and self-blame fed into his already irrational determination to make the expedition a success. Impossible as it will ever be to judge the intimate relationships of others, it seems that this was by no means a loveless marriage, but that Livingstone put duty before family far too often and for too long.

He now decided that the only way to prevent slave traders getting to the Shire Highlands was to patrol a gunboat on Lake Nyasa. He duly paid £6,000 of his own money to purchase an armed steamer and he tried his utmost to assemble and launch it, despite the fact that a drought had left the river level very low. Livingstone's persistence tilted into mania and his men came close to mutiny. The Zambezi Expedition was grounded by a civil war and a famine, and was stuck by a lake that was floating with bloated corpses. This was hardly the mango grove Livingstone had imagined and described so enthusiastically in Cambridge.

Back in Britain, his reputation continued to suffer. *The Times* on 20 January 1863 was damning in its criticism of the expedition: 'We were promised cotton, sugar and indigo … and of course we got none. We were promised converts and not one has been made. In a word, the thousands subscribed … have been productive only of the most fatal results.' In fact, they *had* been productive of a great deal of useful scientific data, but a dispatch from the British government recalling the expedition reached Livingstone on 2 July 1863.

LIVINGSTONE RETURNS TO ENGLAND, 1864–5

In the summer of 1864 Livingstone returned to England to less than a hero's welcome. He did, however, speak at a meeting of the British Association for the Advancement of Science at Bath, and took the opportunity to attack the

Portuguese in Africa. He wrote to his friend Horace Waller, asking him, 'Could you draw a gigantic head – not an ugly one – with a lip ring in it to shew at the theatre tonight?' His injunction to make Africans not look ugly is characteristic, and reflects his position in the argument that was raging over anthropology that was at its height in the mid-1860s. It was a row that pivoted on the visual representation of race, as the Anthropological Society had been set up by James Hunt and the explorer Richard Burton in 1863 as a reaction against the liberal politics and 'picturesque' representation of Africans of the Ethnological Society of London. In fact, Hunt and Burton believed that black Africans were an inferior race, completely unrelated to Caucasians, and were suited to slavery. Livingstone was clearly on the side of the Ethnologicals. In September 1864 he and his daughter Agnes retreated for a while to his friend William Webb's home at Newstead Abbey, near Nottingham. Webb's hunting trophies now decorated the house where Lord Byron had once lived: '[T]here were bundles of elephants' tails hanging up in odd corners, and sheaves of tusks stowed away and half forgotten, whilst the horns and skins of all kinds on walls and floors gave a curious exotic look to the whole house.' Here, Livingstone settled to writing *A Narrative of an Expedition to the Zambesi and its Tributaries*, in which he exonerates himself from blame for the expedition's problems. According to his host, '[H]e detested the necessary writing most heartily.' Some time that summer, Livingstone had received a letter from his eldest son, Robert. In 1863 Robert had set off to join his father at the Zambezi, but he had run out of money in Natal, where he claimed that he was kidnapped and press-ganged into joining the Northern troops in the American Civil War. The letter was a sad one: 'I have changed my name for I am convinced that to bear your name here would lead to further dishonours to it.' On 5 December 1864 Robert died in a Confederate prison camp. He was eighteen years old. Agnes was beside herself with grief for her brother, but Livingstone apparently 'felt the trial acutely ... [but was] too unselfish to permit his grief to affect others unduly'. Neither he nor Agnes knew that in December 1864 Henry Morton Stanley was stationed off Fort Fisher, North Carolina, for the bombardment of one of the last Confederate strongholds of the Atlantic, not far from Robert's lonely deathbed in the prison camp in Salisbury in North Carolina.

LIVINGSTONE RETURNS TO AFRICA TO FIND THE SOURCE OF THE NILE AND GETS LOST, 1865

Livingstone was now determined to find the true source of the Nile and to outsmart Burton. For these Victorians, Africa was as much a mythical realm as a 'real' continent and the quest narratives they produced were imbued with the mystical sense of time travel – as if, in tracing the source of the Nile with Herodotus's description as a guide, they were journeying back to the beginnings of civilisation. On 13 August 1865 Livingstone saw the last of England, sailing to Bombay, where he sold the *Lady Nyasa* and picked up the African servants he had left there early in 1864, including Chuma, Susi and Amoda, all three of whom would stay with him until he died. He also hired a dozen sepoys (Indian soldiers) from the Bombay Marine Battalion and nine boys from the government-run school for freed African slaves at Nasik, not far from Bombay. On the 19 March 1866 the expedition landed on the East African coast, 600 miles north of Quelimane. Livingstone engaged another ten men from the island of

Johanna and his party now numbered thirty-five. This was very small by the standards of the day: most European explorers took more than a hundred men with them. The idea that travelling to Africa meant travelling backwards through time was a very common one then. Africans were seen by many as a different species – lower down the evolutionary scale than white Europeans, and existing in a kind of prehistoric period. Livingstone's attitude to all this was interestingly confused. He did talk paternalistically of the Africans, writing, for example, that 'the natives are at times stupidly perverse', although characteristically he immediately added, 'but we must seem so to them too'. His writing constantly and restlessly mirrors back on to Britain, demanding that his reader understand Africa through empathy: if the British had droughts, he suggests, then they would be as superstitious as the African witchdoctor about rain; and similarly, describing the anklets worn by the women at Linyanti, he remarks, 'The rings are so heavy that the ankles are often blistered by the weight pressing down; but it is the fashion, and is borne as magnanimously as tight lacing and tight shoes among ourselves.' He even suggests that Queen Victoria is a kind of tribal chief. Livingstone uses this rhetorical technique a lot, seemingly because he wants to make his British readers confront how it might feel to be one of the Africans about whom he writes.

Unlike most nineteenth-century missionaries, Livingstone did understand that polygamy was not adultery, and that it had developed as a political rather than merely a sexual practice. He enthusiastically supported the Xhosa and the Khoikhoi peoples who were fighting a war of resistance to European colonial rule in the Cape area. He felt missionaries were morally bound to foster African nationalism in the face of white oppression, and he tried to say so publicly. But his article on the subject was rejected by the British *Quarterly Review* and although he wrote to his brother in America, asking him to help publicise the cause, nothing came of it there either. 'The English as a nation have lost character and honour' in this war, he wrote privately, and he added, approving the fierce resistance of the Xhosa, 'so much for the alleged incapacity of the Hottentots'. Interestingly, he compared the African resistance fighters to the Irish, who 'were for five centuries deemed an inferior race by their English conquerors, but have since vindicated their characters in every department, and more especially in war'.

Of his friend the African chief Sechele, he wrote, 'If such men perish by the advance of civilization, as certain races of animals do before others, it is a pity' – a verdict which is typical of his double and sometimes confusing thinking. But what is much rarer and stranger in Livingstone's writing is the half-formed idea that a linear and hierarchical idea of progress could perhaps be substituted with a more culturally relative model of coexistent difference. In this, too, he differed from Stanley, the younger man, who referred to black Africans routinely as 'sooty faced nigger[s]'. Stanley was always casually, and at times viciously, racist. Livingstone's position was more complicated. He was horrified, for example, by the 'Governor Eyre' scandal of 1865. The British governor of Jamaica had put down a rebellion on the island with extreme violence and British opinion-leaders divided in supporting or vilifying him. Carlyle, Ruskin and Tennyson were among those who supported his actions; Darwin, Mill and John Bright opposed them, along with many working-class radicals. Livingstone was disgusted that Eyre had so many defenders in Britain, saying:

though the majority perhaps are on the side of freedom, large numbers of Englishmen are not slaveholders only because the law forbids the practice. In this proclivity we see a great part of the reason for the frantic sympathy of thousands with the rebels in the great Black war in America ... unquestionably, there existed ... an eager desire that slaveocracy might prosper and the Negro go to the wall. The would-be slaveholders showed their leaning unmistakably in reference to the Jamaica outbreak.

Much has been made by historians recently of a generational split over attitudes to race in Victorian Britain. Some argue that the paternalist model of imperialism in the first half of the century, which figured black people as 'children' to be cared for by whites, gave way in the 1860s to a much harsher idea of black people as a completely different species from whites. It is true that Livingstone and Stanley were a generation apart – Livingstone turned twenty in 1833 and Stanley in 1861 – and so they were certainly formed by very different ideas and experiences of empire and race. But – and surely *much* more importantly – Stanley spent his formative years working for white tradesmen and plantation owners in the American slave-holding South, and so his encounter with slavery was utterly and qualitatively different from Livingstone's encounter at the same age through the Glasgow anti-slavery campaign. Their meeting has been taken as symbolic of the moment when British geographical exploration and anthropological curiosity gave way to an economically driven imperialism that was out for what it could get, in terms of natural resources, labour and profit. There is some truth in this reading, but it only really works if we choose to blot the Stars and Stripes out of the picture of the meeting, ignoring the American side of the story.

And it was the reporter from an American newspaper who shot Livingstone into even greater celebrity status in the summer of 1872. That July Livingstone suddenly burst back into the news on both sides of the Atlantic. Henry Morton Stanley had discovered him, close to death, without supplies, in the town of Ujiji. Stanley fed the sensational story of his encounter with Livingstone in Africa to the newspapers just as they had broken through a technological barrier. In France, America and Britain the newspaper press grew exponentially in size and influence at the end of the 1860s. The new high-speed web printers which used rolls of paper rather than single sheets came into use around 1870. Also, in Britain in 1870 the Government Act, which transferred the telegraph companies to the Post Office, set special press rates that made it cheaper, easier and much faster to report foreign news as it happened.

Most importantly of all, though, after three unsuccessful attempts to link Britain and America by laying a copper cable along the ocean floor, the entrepreneur Cyrus W. Field had succeeded in July 1866. The new transatlantic cable allowed rapid communication across the Anglophone world, and was crucial to the inception of a new global Anglo-American public sphere. Because of the cable, this became the first big story to be reported simultaneously in Britain and America; not only that, but the press was subsequently able to monitor and report how the story was being presented in the 'other' country. This makes it an important episode in the early globalisation of the media. And the story reached into continental Europe too. The famous *Illustrated London News* engraving of the meeting with Stanley, for example, was seen by a great many people in Britain, as the *Illustrated London News* had a circulation five times as big as that of *The Times*. But the same engraving was reproduced around the world, in publications such as the *Graphic, L'Illustration, Illustrazione popolare, Illustrierte Zeitung, Harper's Weekly* and the *Canadian Illustrated News*. The large daily papers were building reputations for their exclusive stories and gained much from the excitement generated – especially before the novelty wore off – of instant communication. The novelty had not worn off in July 1872, when Stanley's story came hot out of Africa and on to breakfast tables across England, continental Europe and America. This was a unique surge in the history of communications technology and Stanley, happening to find himself swept up by it, rode the wave brilliantly.

H. G. Wells, the science fiction writer, was at school in the 1870s and he later remembered occasional and unusual bursts of enthusiasm from his schoolmaster, Mr Morley: '[A]t times he would get excited by his morning paper and then … we would follow the search for Livingstone by Stanley in Darkest Africa.' All over Britain and America people pored over their morning papers and tried to work out Stanley's route. The *Illustrated London News* recommended holiday reading accordingly: 'Anyhow, Africa will be a good deal talked about in the holidays, and Paterfamilias will do well to put an "Afric map" into his "Murray" [travellers' guide].' In one of the greatest newspaper stunts ever, the *New York Herald* journalist had re-established Livingstone's celebrity and made himself famous overnight. Stanley turned his own sudden fame to good account, building himself a high-profile career as African explorer, colonist and – eventually – a British MP. All this he managed on the back of his Livingstone scoop. Stanley's 'discovery' of Livingstone and his subsequent accounts of the explorer's 'Spartan heroism' not only revived but inflated beyond measure the missionary-explorer's reputation both in America and in Europe. During August and September 1872 the Stereoscopic Company brought out photograph sets of Stanley and Livingstone, and Samuel Beeton, husband of the famous cookery writer, was quick to offer a cheap book on Livingstone and Stanley 'with portraits'. In America too there was a revival of interest in Livingstone: he appeared, for example, in Evert Augustus Duyckinck's *Portrait Gallery of Eminent Men and Women of Europe and America*, which came out in parts between 1872 and 1874. Over the next year there were numerous popular and sensational lectures on Stanley and Livingstone in Britain: at the Royal Polytechnic in London in October 1872 a lecture on Stanley's search for Livingstone featured alongside 'the Valjean Brothers in their wonderful Athletic Feats; new Ghost Illusion, [and] The White Lady of Avenal'. It was precisely the entry of African exploration into popular culture in this way that alarmed the gentlemen of the establishment and particularly the Fellows of the RGS. Livingstone, himself a Fellow, was popping up everywhere and such promiscuity did not seem quite gentlemanly. For example, Livingstone's *Missionary Travels* was being quoted, probably without his permission, in advertisements for a patent nostrum called REVALENTA ARABICA, one of the 'mysterious watchwords' Dickens noticed plastered on placard advertisements all over London. In 1872, after the Education Act of 1870 that made elementary schooling compulsory in Britain, 'an account of a flooded prairie in Africa by Dr Livingstone' was included in the School Board Reader (Level 5), so that the explorer was soon to be encountered by every child in the country. By the 1880s and 1890s, large orders were being placed by the school authorities for a new cheap, two-volume edition of *Missionary Travels* and Livingstone's second travel book issued by Murray's.

Madame Tussaud's famous wax museum in London reacted early to Livingstone's fame and Bernard Tussaud had modelled the wax likeness of the explorer with his own hands in 1872. The 'PORTRAIT MODEL' of Livingstone was being advertised for view in the newspapers just a few weeks after Stanley's story broke. The 1873 catalogue records that waxworks of Livingstone, Stanley and Stanley's black servant Kalulu, were on permanent exhibition. The likeness of Livingstone was a good one, by the account of William Webb's daughter Augusta Fraser, who knew him well: 'Dr Livingstone was in face very like his portraits, but (although it sounds as if I must be a Philistine to say so) he resembled still more his waxen effigy at Madame Tussaud's, and I well remember the start of surprise with which I greeted the well-known figure when I first saw it a few years later.' After Livingstone's death, the museum also acquired 'valuable relics belonging to the great explorer', which included 'his now famous "crockery", his bed, [and] his left-hand glove, which was one of the things which led to his certain identification'. As is clear from Fraser's worry about being thought a 'philistine' for mentioning it, Tussaud's was a truly popular museum. One contemporary reviewer noted, '[a]ll classes, educated and uneducated, old and young' filed past the wax effigy of Livingstone.

People of all classes, too, turned out in their thousands to line the streets around Westminster Abbey on the day of Livingstone's funeral in April 1874. After refusing to accompany Stanley back to Europe, Livingstone set off once more on his Nile quest. But his bowels – always his weak point

– began to make him seriously ill and he was soon being carried on a stretcher by his servants. Eventually, they built him a hut to lie in, and there he died, in Chitambo's village, in May 1873. When his body was returned to Britain in 1874, his funeral was a national public event of a kind that had not been seen on the streets of London since the funeral of Wellington in 1852. Newspapers covered the event in almost obsessive detail and most also commented approvingly on the decent and sober behaviour of the crowds. The Scottish Livingstone was buried in a coffin of English oak under the floor in the centre of the nave of the Abbey. On his tombstone his 'last words' were inlaid in brass: 'All I can add in my solitude, is, may heaven's rich blessing come down on every one – American, English, Turk – who will help to heal this open sore of the world.' By the open sore, he meant slavery. But, in fact, Livingstone did not write 'in my solitude', he really wrote 'in my loneliness', making this a much bleaker and less hopeful statement. His unofficial canonisation would lead to many such creative edits of the actual words of his letters and journals. His last letters to the Webbs were despairing and bitter as their daughter remembered: '[F]or ill, with the sickness of hope deferred, even Livingstone's great brave heart had at times given way to the horrors of abandonment, and in these letters he poured out the bitterness of his soul in a manner he had never done before.'

Needless to say, these letters were not published in the *Last Journals* (1874). The editor, Livingstone's friend Horace Waller, assiduously expunged anything that he thought might create an impression of the explorer as less than a manly and muscular Christian. Waller, a minister and a prominent campaigner against slavery, wanted to promote both missionary work and abolition. It is this Livingstone, the muscular Christian, who appears in the *Boy's Own Paper* alongside Stanley: the Livingstone who is willing, the boy readers are told, to 'sacrifice home and comfort, and life itself, if haply he might open up the vast centre of Africa to Christian light and civilisation', and who would later be recruited by Baden-Powell to serve as an example to young masculinity in his 1908 series *Scouting for Boys: A Handbook for Instruction in Good Citizenship*. 'I suppose every British boy wants to help his country in some way or other,' announces Baden-Powell, and Livingstone appears at the beginning of the book as an example of those who 'give up everything, their personal comforts and desires, in order to get their work done. They do not do all this for their own amusement, but because it is their duty to their King, fellow countrymen, or employers.'

Following so fast upon his rediscovery, Livingstone's death and bizarre state funeral created another media frenzy. As far away as Russia speeches were made about Livingstone's greatness. More Livingstone merchandise poured out, along with much poetry of questionable merit. Herr Reichardt wrote a new song called 'Dreams of Home', which was published just after the funeral on 25 April. The lyrics by W. Henderson played upon Livingstone's supposed longing for his 'homeland' as he died far away in Africa. *The Times* summed up this feeling: '[I]t was impossible to look on this solemn popular triumph unmoved; for the mind of the spectator could not help insensibly reverting to that rude and lonely African hut where nearly a year ago England's greatest and noblest hearted traveller drew his last breath.' In fact, Stanley remembered, '[T]he Doctor remarked that he could never pass through an African forest, with its solemn stillness and serenity, without wishing to be buried quietly under the dead leaves, where he would be sure to rest undisturbed. In England there was no elbow-room, the graves were often desecrated', so maybe Livingstone's last thoughts were not, in fact, of 'home'. The National Portrait Gallery in London used to operate a 'ten-year rule', which meant that, in the nineteenth century, it did not usually acquire portraits of people until they had been dead for ten years at least. Livingstone's celebrity was such that this rule was suspended in his case and a drawing of the missionary-explorer by Joseph Bonomi was exhibited by the gallery in 1874. Just after the funeral a bust of Livingstone was completed and set in a roundel on the front of the newly opened Foreign and Colonial Office buildings. He can still be seen from the top of a double-decker bus going down Whitehall. The other busts in the same series are of *Cook, Drake, Franklin, Wilberforce* and *Albert*. A statue of Victoria herself sits on top of the building. By 1876 there were roads being named after Livingstone in the newly built suburbs that were unfolding around the railway lines into London – in Norwood, Walthamstow and Clapham. It is difficult to reconstruct the emotion unleashed by the idea of Livingstone in the nineteenth century, but his appeal as a 'working-class-hero' caught the imagination of the public of the 1870s, and this helped to ensure the lasting fame of both Livingstone and Stanley.

THE LATE VICTORIAN LIVINGSTONE

Livingstone's myth lived on. Horace Waller's carefully edited version of Livingstone's *Last Journals* appeared in 1874, and in the later nineteenth century biographies of the missionary doctor proliferated, continuing Waller's and Stanley's work of hagiography. By the turn of the century the LMS was using a magic lantern show entitled *The Life and Work of David Livingstone* to inspire the young with the example of a man who 'made the way for liberty in Africa by his own daring and suffering'. A steady stream of over a hundred full-length biographies appeared between Livingstone's death and the Second World War. And that is not counting the numerous biographical articles in the newspapers and periodicals. The two standard biographies to appear in the Victorian period, one by Dr William Garden Blaikie (1880) and one by Thomas Hughes, the author of *Tom Brown's Schooldays* (1889), dwelt much on Livingstone's death scene. Livingstone was supposed to have been found dead by his servants, kneeling as if in prayer by his bed. In fact, close attention to the manuscript notebook in which Waller took dictation of Susi's and Chuma's memories of Livingstone's death reveals that they found him in a kneeling position on the bed, not by it, with his head buried in the pillow – not quite such a prayerful attitude as Blaikie and Hughes would have us believe: 'Dr when he died had on trousers The boy said he fell asleep & when he woke he still saw him in this position & got alarmed he was kneeling on his bed with his head on the pillow'. And an account by another of his servants, Carus Farrar, has it differently, saying that Majuara, the servant who slept with Livingstone, left the hut to go to the loo, 'but on his return again he found the Dr fallen on the ground already expired'. Livingstone died of an intestinal blockage and his hunched position may of course have been a reaction to a spasm of pain. Nevertheless, Blaikie's 1880 biography assumes extraordinary access into Livingstone's last thoughts:

But he had died in the act of prayer – prayer offered in that reverential attitude about which he was always so particular; commending his own spirit, with all his dear ones, as was his wont, into the hands of his Saviour; and commending AFRICA – his own dear Africa – with all her woes and sins and wrongs, to the Avenger of the oppressed and the Redeemer of the lost.

LIVINGSTONE IN THE TWENTIETH CENTURY

The Birthplace

In November 1925 a Scottish pastor, James Macnair, went in search of Livingstone's birthplace. What he discovered shocked him: the building was 'a slum, [and] housed the type of tenant it deserved'. Livingstone's heroic reputation lived on and an old woman was making a small income by showing the 'little birthroom' to the occasional visitors who braved the squalor, but 'the general surroundings were so disreputable that no Scotsman could take an overseas friend there, without an acute sense of shame'. Macnair decided to appeal to 'the Scottish people' and to try and save Livingstone's birthplace for the nation. 'It was soon found that the humblest and the highest of the land could be approached with equal confidence in his name and that every help that could be, would be gladly given.' One of the keys to Livingstone's enduring popularity as a national hero was his cross-class appeal. Despite the General Strike in May 1926, which made money scarce for ordinary people, contributions came in, mostly from Scotland and mostly from private, middle-income donors. The idea was to create a museum around Livingstone's birthplace which would become 'a shrine in which the great tradition should remain firmly founded'.

On 5 October 1929 the Livingstone Birthplace Museum at Blantyre was opened by HRH the Duchess of York, and the ceremony, which included a Church of Scotland service with 10,000 in the congregation, was broadcast by the BBC – another indication of how important Livingstone was then deemed to be as a Scottish hero. After the Duchess of York had formally unlocked the door of Livingstone's birth room, Macnair made a speech, saying, 'The door just opened is narrow and the stair it leads to, stiff and difficult – fit symbol of the life of the great man born there.' Given that Livingstone left Scotland at the age of twenty-three and rarely returned in adult life, it seems curious that such significance should be attached to his birthplace. Partly, of course, the museum plan was a way of reappropriating the British myth of Livingstone for Scotland at a time when Scottish nationalist feeling was strong – the National Party of Scotland was founded in 1928 and what has become known as the 'Scottish Renaissance' was gathering speed between the wars. Even in 1913, the centenary of Livingstone's birth, Hamish MacCunn, a Scottish composer, had written a cantata called 'Livingstone the Pilgrim'. Livingstone was useful to Scottish nationalism because he symbolically reconciled the differences between Highland and Lowland Scotland (his father was from the island of Ulva off Mull, but Livingstone grew up near Glasgow). But Livingstone was also celebrated as an exemplar of the pursuit of knowledge under difficulties – and central to the concept of the Blantyre museum was its display of his conspicuously humble but respectable origins. The museum pivoted around 'the little room, ten by fourteen feet in size, in which on the 19th March, 1813, David was born'. Eight wall panels in tempera told 'the well-known stories of Livingstone's strenuous youth; stories that are part of Scotland's heritage'.

Scotland also of course had a particular relationship with the British Empire, as many of its administrators were Scots. Nevertheless, it is difficult to say just how aware of the Empire David Livingstone and his contemporaries would have been as they were growing up. Contact with foreign places seems to have come to Livingstone through his chapel and its connections with English and American missionary societies rather than through newspapers, which he does not record reading in his youth. It was probably more a construction of the 1920s and 1930s that Livingstone's 'strenuous youth' was particularly connected with his success as an African explorer. The Blantyre museum is now run by the National Trust for Scotland and has recently undergone a £1.2 million redevelopment. Today it places less emphasis on Livingstone's strenuous youth than on his place in Scottish heritage culture – its brochure offers '[g]uided tours ... with costumed historical characters'.

In August 1939, on the eve of the declaration of war by Britain and France on Germany on 3 September, an American film called *Stanley and Livingstone* was released by Twentieth-Century Fox. It starred Spencer Tracy in the lead role as Stanley and Sir Cedric Hardwicke as Livingstone. This was very much a film about Stanley rather than about Livingstone. The film opens as a Western, in 1870 in Wyoming Territory, where Stanley is discovered outdoing the government's peace commissioners and winning an interview with the 'Indians'. The backwoodsman Jeff Slocum, whom Stanley meets in Wyoming, accompanies him throughout the film, and it is Slocum's expertise in bush warfare with 'Indians' that later helps them escape the attack of African 'tribes'. The suggested parallels between savage native peoples are obvious, and despite the film's two or three references to slavery, black Africans are figured throughout as bloodthirsty and savage. The British, instead, are languid and ineffectual, broken by Africa. Livingstone is inspirational but an idealist and a visionary, whereas Stanley is thoroughly American in his purposeful energy. That is until the last scene, which takes place – improbably – in the Brighton Pavilion at a meeting of the RGS, when Stanley suddenly reveals his 'English' origins and appeals to his 'fellow countrymen', thus dramatising the connection between the two Anglo-Saxon nations. When Livingstone's death is announced during this meeting, his last request is relayed to Stanley: 'My son, the torch has fallen from my hand. Come and relight it.' Stanley goes off to finish Livingstone's work – 'I can at least try to finish the work he started' – but the shots of Stanley's expedition marching across a superimposed map of 'The Congo' and the soundtrack ending 'with the cross of Jesus going on before' do not make it clear exactly which work of Livingstone's he is supposed to be fulfilling, exploration or mission. In fact, Stanley was never a missionary. But the film refuses to reflect on the differences between the two men, and to an American audience in 1939 its message is clear. The Americans and the British are Christian brothers in freeing the world from darkness, while the British are well meaning but a bit hopeless and might need help from their purposeful, energetic and youthful American friends. The writer Graham Greene noticed the film's privileging of American energy over British formality: 'Mr Tracy [Stanley] is always a human being, but Sir Cedric [Livingstone] is an elocution lesson, a handclasp.'

By the mid-twentieth century much of Livingstone's religious and missionary context had fallen out of the story, leaving a secularised *Boy's Own* narrative of adventuring and discovering. But his story was still told. In May 1951 Livingstone was subsumed into the history of British discovery and exploration in the Dome of Discovery at the Festival of Britain. The Dome exhibited 'the spirit of adventure and discovery which has prompted the British people all along'.

Here, interestingly, a highly secularised Livingstone was written into a narrative about the development of British science, a narrative which culminated in space travel: 'It is our scientists who have inherited the cloaks of such great explorers as Drake, Cook and Livingstone,' said Ian Cox, who was Director of Science for the Festival. While 'Chocolate Coins of the British Empire' were advertised as 'The Ideal Gift for your Children', the history of British colonisation was deliberately played down by the exhibits and instead the interdependency and communication between Britain and her former colonies was stressed, the British Commonwealth being represented on London's South Bank in 1951 by 'the symbol of the physical links that tie the Commonwealth countries together – sea lanes, the routes of aircraft, railways, cables and long-distance radio'. This would have pleased Livingstone, whose colonial fantasies were mostly about channels of communication linking Britain and Africa. There was a kind of ellipse or gap in the discussion in the Dome of Discovery, though – no mention of Stanley, for example, and no mention of the brutality of the late-nineteenth-century 'Scramble for Africa' – which makes this an eloquent example of history being reframed. In London in 1951, at a difficult moment for British imperialism, much of the original significance of Livingstone's story became emptied out.

The British Empire had left Palestine and given up South Africa to the Commonwealth immediately after the Second World War. India became independent in 1947, the Irish Free State became the Irish Republic in 1949, and Britain was to be humiliated by the Suez Crisis in 1956. The years from 1951 to 1964 witnessed the end of the Victorian imperial project for Britain. Just three years before the Festival of Britain, the *Empire-Windrush*, the first government-sponsored ship carrying West Indians to settle in the UK, had docked at Tilbury on 22 June 1948. The Empire was coming home in a way that was to transform race relations and what it meant to be British over the next fifty years. In 1953, in the weak twilight of the British Empire, the Secretary of State for the Colonies, Oliver Lyttelton, unveiled a bronze statue of Livingstone by T. B. Huxley-Jones. The statue was set in a niche in the RGS building, where it can still be seen today. Lyttelton said, 'When we look back upon the nineteenth century … we see that it was an age of great men. Foremost among them, we see the historic virtues of their age epitomised in David Livingstone.' Livingstone was no longer missionary, geographer or anti-slavery campaigner: all these roles were now subsumed into a 'great man' and a representative of the Victorian age.

Madame Tussaud's Waxworks Museum had – and still has – a strict policy of topicality in its exhibits: when a personality falls out of public notice, the waxwork is removed and melted. So it is remarkable that Livingstone survived unmelted into the 1930s and beyond, and latterly was exhibited in a group with Shackleton and Scott of the famous 1912 Arctic expedition, demonstrating the way in which Livingstone's story had by then become tangled with that other story of great British martyrdom and heroic failure. A

8. The wax model of Dr Livingstone (far left) was displayed with models of Shackleton and Scott in Madame Tussaud's wax-work museum in the early twentieth century.

cartoon that appeared in the *Daily Mirror* on 27 December 1968, in celebration of the return of Apollo 8 to earth that day, has Livingstone as part of the group of 'The Great

Adventurers', along with Cook, Drake, Scott and Columbus, who are giving up the pedestal to Borman, Lovell and Anders. In 1973, on the centenary of Livingstone's death, the GPO issued a series of four 'British Explorers' stamps and Stanley and Livingstone each appeared on the 3p stamps. The Clydesdale Bank had put an image of Livingstone on its £10 note in 1972. Tim Jeal's classic and invaluable biography of Livingstone also appeared in 1973, and substituted scrupulous archival research for the conventional genuflections. His pioneering work was followed by other more questioning biographies. Judith Listowel published *The Other Livingstone* in 1974, for example, in which she accuses Livingstone of attempting to suppress the contribution of other explorers in his accounts of his travels. Oliver Ransford's *David Livingstone: The Dark Interior* came out in 1978, suggesting that Livingstone had developed manic depression by the time he was forty and was a difficult and unpleasant man.

LIVINGSTONE IN THE TWENTY-FIRST CENTURY

In Africa in 2002 the enormous bronze statue of David Livingstone overlooking the Victoria Falls, now in Zimbabwe, was defaced by supporters of Robert Mugabe's regime, who were clearly not in agreement with the inscription 'the light of Africa, bringer of the gospel, unshackler of slaves', and perhaps were reacting against Livingstone's place in the iconography of local racism. The statue was modelled by William Reid Dick and erected in 1934 in order to celebrate Livingstone's 'discovery' of the Falls in 1855. At that time, Livingstone and Cecil Rhodes were viewed as the joint founders of settler power in the region. This was the period that saw the establishment of the David Livingstone

Memorial Museum and the Rhodes–Livingstone Institute in what was then Northern Rhodesia. The 1937 museum handbook tells us that the name of the institute 'commemorates the two men who, in their different ways, have wielded so great an influence on the history of the Territory'. In 2004 the Zambian chief of the Leya people, who live on the other side of Victoria Falls, was reported as requesting that his people take custody of the statue. While most of the places named by European explorers and missionaries in the nineteenth century have long since reverted to their original African names, the Leya people hold on to Livingstone as the name of their town 'out of a deep respect', he said. Now that Zimbabwe is too dangerous for white tourists, Zambia is of course making capital from western tourism and this may explain some of the 'respect' for Livingstone – but it cannot be the whole story. If Livingstone represented nothing but white oppression to the majority of Zambian people, it is unlikely that their chief would be able to speak publicly of their loyalty to him in this way. Indeed, one of Livingstone's 'afterlives' in Africa has been as a powerful symbol of abolition and an advocate for slaves. In western Uganda, for example, the minority Bakonjo people invoked his memory in their protests against the Toro aristocracy, their overlords, appealing to British liberal sentiment and criticising the injustices of local, colonial inequality.

Livingstone's legacy in Africa is very complicated. Dr Blaikie ended his hagiographic biography in 1880 by representing Livingstone as the founding father of modern Africa: 'When ... generation after generation of intelligent Africans look back on its beginnings, as England looks back on the days of King Alfred, Ireland of St. Patrick, Scotland of St. Columba, or the United States of George Washington, the name that is to be encircled by them with brightest honour is that of DAVID LIVINGSTONE.' And modern historian John MacKenzie has gone so far as to suggest that 'Livingstone somehow made the transition from the apostle of empire to a patron saint of nationalism', which may perhaps be too grand a claim in both directions, although it is true that the African nationalist and leader of a black uprising during the First World War, John Cimlembwe, had a copy of Livingstone's biography in his possession, and some African countries continued to honour Livingstone officially even after they became independent. Of course, for Livingstone, Christianity was much more important as the index of group identity than nationhood.

After independence from Britain in 1964, Zambia issued a set of stamps in 1973, the centenary of Livingstone's death, showing iconic scenes from his life: the 'discovery' of the Falls, freeing slaves, preaching, doctoring and a picture of the tree under which his heart is buried. Stamps issued in 1973 in Burundi, which won independence from UN Trusteeship under Belgian administration in 1962, show the famous meeting between Livingstone and Stanley.

In 1972, the South African writer Nadine Gordimer published a collection of short stories under the title *Livingstone's Companions*. In the title story the journalist-narrator muses upon Livingstone's death: '[I]t must have been hell to die here, in this unbearable weight of beauty not shared with the known world, licked in the face by the furred tongue of this heat.' He watches an African hotel boy picking up bottle tops and cigarette butts and thinks, '[T]his was the enlightenment the discoverers had brought the black man in the baggage he portered for them on his head.' We may well wonder, when reading about Livingstone and Stanley, where

African history is. The African-Caribbean Canadian novelist
Marlene Nourbese Philip has described this silence:

David Livingstone, *Dr* David Livingstone, 1813–73
– Scottish, not English, and one of the first Europeans
to cross the Kalahari – *with* the help of Bushmen; was
shown the Zambezi by the indigenous African and 'discovered' it; was shown the falls of Mosioatunya – the
smoke that thunders – by the indigenous African, 'discovered' it and renamed it. Victoria Falls. Then he set out
to 'discover' the source of the Nile and was himself 'discovered' by Stanley – 'Dr Livingstone, I presume?' And
History. Stanley and Livingstone – white fathers of the
continent. Of silence.

This silence is a difficult one to puncture. Any European
account of Livingstone and Stanley will necessarily run the
risk of reinforcing that silence, and of ignoring once more
that giant act of forgetting that we are asked to accomplish
in remembering Livingstone and Stanley. But the point is not
finally whether Livingstone's African porters are remembered, it is that an immensely complicated African history
has been collapsed into so simple an image.

When we are asked to think of Livingstone, we are asked
to think of the Africa that Europeans pictured in 1857 with
'a vast extent of its area which can only be represented by
a vacant space upon our maps'. Throughout Livingstone's
own narratives, instances of this kind of selective blindness
abound. One particularly striking example occurs in his
Missionary Travels, which includes a lithograph, entitled 'Lake
Ngami, Discovered by Oswell, Murray, and Livingstone'
– on the lake there are Africans in canoes. And on the facing

page is written: 'We were informed by the Bayeíye, who live on the lake, that, when the annual inundation begins ...' To Oswell, Murray and Livingstone, the Africans were not in the landscape, they *were* the landscape, and so could not see it or own it in the same way that Europeans could. Livingstone's memory was certainly perpetuated by the missionary activity in Africa after his death and well into the twentieth century. Missionaries, in search of their own founding father, turned to Livingstone. All over Africa, Livingstone's biography was translated into African languages, and pamphlets were sold and distributed by missions. His life was used as a model for African students. For example, in 1930 prospective elementary school teachers at Tumutumu in Kenya had to write an array of short biographical essays in their qualifying examinations; seven possible topics were chosen by their headmaster and 'David Livingstone' was one of them. Many thousands of Africans were and still are educated in mission schools, and to the missionaries who came after him, Livingstone became an important block in the monumentalisation of their own founding moment. In 1913, for example, the Universities' Mission Society wrote to a donor thanking him for a gift of portraits of David Livingstone and asking for something 'which definitely associates him with the Universities Mission & which would allow us to explain that connection on the label'. Evangelical Christianity is now growing faster in Africa, Asia and Latin America than in the West. But the exponential growth of Christianity in Africa has nothing to do with Livingstone. In fact, the earlier Jesuit missions were much more effective, as he himself acknowledged – '[t]he Jesuits, in Africa at last, were wiser in their generation than we,' – and North American Pentecostalism in the late nineteenth and early twentieth centuries also contributed hugely. But of course the real question is what it was that Africans found in Christian thought that was so useful to them. Whatever their significance, Livingstone and Stanley are still around in Africa. For example, in Bagamoyo, now in Tanzania and formerly an ivory and slave port whose name in Swahili means 'throw down your heart' – an expression of the despair of the slaves brought here for export – there is a small museum at the church where Livingstone's body was laid briefly by his servants on their epic journey back to the coast. Almost anywhere in Africa that Livingstone so much as passed through will have its memorial, and it is difficult to move around Victoria Falls as a tourist without being constantly reminded of Livingstone and Stanley by hotel names (the Stanley and Livingstone; Chuma House; Sussi Lodge; the Royal Livingstone; the Stanley Safari Lodge, etc.) and there is even a 'Flight of the Angels' helicopter trip over the Falls, quoting Livingstone's celebrated description in *Missionary Travels*.

And Livingstone and Stanley still circulate in popular fiction. *Into Africa: The Epic Adventures of Stanley and Livingstone* appeared in 2003. This thrills-and-spills retelling is by Martin Dugard, a former sports journalist and adventure-racer who has writen on subjects such as the last voyage of Columbus and the Tour de France. In 2004 American science-fiction writer Robin Wayne Bailey published a story called 'The Terminal Solution', which imagines an alternative history in which David Livingstone brings AIDS in 1864 from 'the darkest heart of Africa' to Victorian London. The pulling together of the nineteenth-century fantasy of Africa (Livingstone) and the twenty-first (AIDS) is perhaps more revealing than Bailey intended it to be of the way in which western culture recycles its old stereotypes. In an interview, Bailey said, 'the entire story resulted from a dream.' Certainly such stereotypes often function at the level of the unconscious. The old fear of possible contamination by the 'savage' – or the revenge of the colonised – is reinflected through the fear of a modern epidemic that respects no boundaries.

The Victorian encounter with Africa still underpins some of the most fundamental of the ways in which we figure ourselves in what we now like to call the 'developed' world. The meeting of these two Anglo-Saxon men in 'darkest Africa' has become so iconic because of its intersection with a particular political moment and with a particular moment in media history. The frayed state of Anglo-American relations in the early 1870s drew international attention to the incident, and the Atlantic cable allowed a dialogue between American and British newspapers that created one of the first 'celebrity moments'. So much of the enduring iconic power of the meeting derives from the suspicion and uneasiness it produced at the time – a suspicion and uneasiness that were channelled into laughter. Many in 1872 thought there was something fishy about the story – that it was so sensational it might turn out to be a fraud or a lie. The reason that it entered popular culture so immediately and intravenously was this very iffiness – because people were not entirely sure whether it had really happened or not. It entered the culture at the level of representation and reactions to it indicate a public understanding of the manipulations of the media that historians sometimes tend to miss. The ultimate irony is that the meeting has survived as iconic of a kind of absent-minded British imperialism precisely because it was first *ironic*. In the 1870s it was in fact used to question and to

poke fun at grand notions of 'empire', but slowly the irony
has dropped out and we are left with just those two men in
the jungle clearing.

2

THE MEETING

'At last the sublime hour has arrived! – our dreams, our hopes, our anticipations are now about to be realised!' On what may have been Friday 27 October 1871, or a couple of weeks later – both Livingstone and Stanley were confused about quite what day it was – Stanley recalls walking into Ujiji and, to his surprise, finding himself addressed in English by 'a man dressed in a long white shirt, with a turban of American sheeting around his woolly head'. A conversation follows:

'Who the mischief are you?'
'I am Susi, the servant of Dr Livingstone,' said he, smiling, and showing a gleaming row of teeth.
'What! Is Dr Livingstone here?'
'Yes, sir.'
'In this village?'
'Yes, sir.'
'Are you sure?'
'Sure, sure, sir. Why, I leave him just now.'
'Good morning, sir,' said another voice.
'Hallo,' said I, 'is this another one?'
'Yes, sir.'
'Well, what is your name?'

> 'My name is Chumah, sir.'
> 'What! Are you Chumah, the friend of Wekotani?'
> 'Yes, sir.'
> 'And is the Doctor well?'
> 'Not very well, sir.'
> 'Where has he been so long?'
> 'In Manyuema.'
> 'Now you, Susi, run, and tell the Doctor I am coming.'
> 'Yes, sir.' And he darted off like a madman.

Stanley had endured a miserable and at times desperate journey to reach this point, suffering twenty-three episodes of fever and dysentery, and near-mutiny from his men. He was also living in constant fear lest Livingstone should run away from him if he got wind of the relief expedition – 'Was HE still there? Had HE heard of my coming? Would HE fly?' John Kirk, the British Consul at Zanzibar, had warned him, '"[H]e hates to have anyone with him."' Now it seemed that he had finally caught up with Livingstone – a piece of astonishing luck – and Stanley was bursting with excitement:

> What would I not have given for a bit of friendly wilderness wherein I might vent my joy in some mad freaks, such as idiotically biting my hand, twisting a somersault, slashing at trees, in order to allay those exciting feelings that were well-nigh uncontrollable. My heart beats fast, but I must not let my face betray my emotions, lest it shall detract from the dignity of the white man appearing under such extraordinary circumstances.

This is the beginning of his elaborate explanation for why

he uttered the words he was never going to be allowed to forget: 'Dr Livingstone, I presume?'

Jumping around and turning somersaults was exactly the kind of behaviour for which Stanley had constantly derided his African companions, and he was determined to keep up 'the dignity of the white man'. But it is worth remembering that Stanley was writing this account after his return to Europe, when he had discovered to his horror that 'Dr Livingstone, I presume?' had instantly become a comic catchphrase and was being bandied around in music halls, clubs and taverns. The page of Stanley's journal describing his encounter with Livingstone has been torn out, so it is, of course, possible that he never actually uttered the phrase, but he reported that he did to the *New York Herald* in dispatches of 15 July and 10 August 1872, and so he had to stick by the story, whether it was true or not, upon his return. He explains: 'I would have run to him – only I was a coward in the presence of such a mob – would have embraced him, only, he being an Englishman, I did not know how he would receive me.' In an anxious footnote, he cites a precedent from Kinglake's *Eöthen*, in which the famous travel writer describes encountering a fellow Englishman in the middle of the solitary desert: he touched his cap to him and 'we passed each other as if we had passed on Bond Street'. Much of the hilarity with which Stanley's line was received in England and America pivoted on the seeming incongruity of the formality of the greeting in what people pictured as an accidental meeting in the solitary wilderness of Africa.

In fact, Ujiji was not, as we have seen, a solitary wilderness, and the meeting was not entirely accidental. Stanley and Livingstone did not suddenly trip over one another in a jungle clearing. Stanley was pretty sure of Livingstone's presence in the town before he descended, to the point that he and his men were already 'peer[ing] into the palms and try[ing] to make out in which hut or house lives the white man with the grey beard'. Stanley had changed his 'white flannels' in preparation and his 'Hawkes' patent cork solar topee' had been freshly chalked. Stanley's caravan marched into Ujiji, with the 'American flag borne aloft', after firing a volley of shots to announce their imminent arrival. Ujiji was a sizeable cosmopolitan town, with a 'Broadway' and a market square which Stanley dubbed the 'Place de Ujiji' and which he remembers as thronging with 'ramblers and loungers' in the long, warm evenings. Susi had gone ahead with the news of his arrival and Stanley found Livingstone surrounded by 'the great Arab magnates of Ujiji – Mohammed bin Sali, Sayd bin Majid, Abid bin Suliman, Mohammed bin Gharib, and others'. The occasion was, in fact, highly formal. Rather than a clearing in the jungle, Stanley met Livingstone in a town that he did not entirely understand, and a certain degree of deference both to Livingstone and to the 'great Arab magnates' on their own territory was probably perfectly appropriate, even if Stanley afterwards berated himself for 'cowardice and false pride' in being so reserved in his first words to Livingstone.

Stanley was never to understand exactly why everyone thought 'Dr Livingstone, I presume?' was so side-splittingly funny. His morbid self-doubt made him assume that they were laughing at him, because he was American and not a real English 'gentleman', so had somehow failed to get it quite right. 'I make enemies every day of my life,' he once remarked. Probably, Stanley's own reflex of racism made it difficult for him to unpick the profound racism that underpins the joke. People thought the line was funny because they imagined Livingstone and Stanley must have been the *only* two white men in Africa, so who else could Livingstone possibly have been? But the joke goes deeper than this. They also assumed that there must be no civilisation, and therefore no civility, in Africa. In fact, as Livingstone and Stanley both knew, there were complicated codes of etiquette and civility everywhere in Africa. For example, Livingstone understood very well that black Africans 'knew that little business could be transacted without a liberal amount of time for palaver'.

Stanley remembers that he and Livingstone raised their hats to one another and then 'we both grasp[ed] hands'. The handshake as a form of greeting, which seemed so 'English' to the British and therefore so comically incongruous in 'darkest Africa', had in fact already been imitated and appropriated by supposedly 'uncivilised' black Africans. Edward Young in 1867 records the delight of the Makololo in greeting him: 'Shaking hands had been instituted in former times in lieu of native clapping; and now nothing would do but that man, woman, and child should go through the ceremony.' Even in the early 1920s a correspondent of the *Daily Telegraph*, reporting from the expedition making the film *Livingstone* in Africa, was capable of breathtaking racism when describing African greeting practices. He describes 'a huge coal-black negro, riding a bicycle, and wearing a brand-new silk opera hat. He dismounts as we pass, and removes the hat with a flourish and a low bow. It is as startlingly incongruous as if one met a gorilla casually strolling along Piccadilly.' Modern anthropologists recognise the discomfort of these moments of 'second encounter': when the coloniser sees him- or herself reflected back in the behaviour of the colonised. But acts of African civility are rendered almost entirely invisible in these nineteenth-century European accounts that persistently represent African good manners as some kind of comic circus act. This helps explain why Anglo-American readers thought Stanley's 'presuming' was so hilarious – two white men surrounded by uncivil grunting 'savages' would be expected to fall upon each other's necks. The *Philadelphia Post*, for example, reported, 'There is something almost sublime in the meeting between Livingstone and Stanley in the deserts of Africa. The noble old man was in the midst of barbarians, poor and alone.' In fact, Stanley and Livingstone were two white men surrounded by – and dependent on – a group of extremely polite and helpful black and Arab Africans.

To Stanley's relief, Livingstone did not appear to be the antisocial bear that he had imagined. He was delighted to be 'found', very talkative and extremely grateful to Stanley for his trouble. Stanley describes himself as bedazzled by the 'wonderful man', so much so that he even forgot the job at hand for a while: 'I was too much engrossed to take my note-book out, and to begin to stenograph his story.' Then, rather than a journalist, he was required to become a news-paper: 'Shortly I found myself enacting the part of an annual periodical to him. There was no need of exaggeration – of any penny-a-line news, or any sensationalism. The world had witnessed and experienced much in the last few years.' He ran Livingstone through the main headlines, dwelling particularly on the ongoing Franco-Prussian War. 'I never fancied myself more of a newspaperman than I did when at Ujiji with such an attentive listener as Livingstone.' Stanley could not help crowing a little when he handed over a bag of mail to Livingstone that had taken a year to get from Zanzibar to Ujiji. 'How long, I wonder, had it remained at Unyanyembe had I not been despatched into Central Africa in search of the great traveller?' Livingstone was too excited by Stanley's arrival to read more than a couple of letters from his children. Their Arab hosts sent round presents of choice food to the house, and Livingstone, a mere 'ruckle of bones', who claimed all he had recently managed to digest was cups of tea, tucked in heartily to a plate of pancakes. '"You have brought me new life. You have brought me new life,"' he kept repeating, in between mouthfuls. He had not seen another white man since March 1866. Stanley got out the 'bottle of Sillery champagne' and two silver goblets that he had had carried all the way from Bagamoyo in the hope of meeting with just this occasion. When this scene was reproduced in the 1925 *Livingstone* film it caused some consternation, as Scottish prohibitionists objected to the Doctor being shown drinking alcohol. But drink alcohol he did. The afternoon dwindled pleasantly into evening, and in the excitement of their conversation Livingstone never got round to asking Stanley why exactly he was there.

THE STARS AND STRIPES AND THE *NEW YORK HERALD*

'The American flag at the head of a caravan told me the nationality of the stranger,' Livingstone remembered in his account of the meeting, and the inhabitants of Ujiji recognised it too, shouting, '"Bindera Merikani!" – the American flag!' The Stars and Stripes had been given to Stanley by Mrs Webb, the wife of the American Consul at Zanzibar, and Stanley ordered his servants to 'Unfurl the flags' as they prepared to descend into Ujiji – both the Stars and Stripes and the flag of Zanzibar, which brought up the rear of the party. As would happen again in Stanley's exploring career, an expedition that was in fact the private enterprise of a

commercial newspaper marched under a national flag, blur-
ring the boundaries between government and press in just
the ways that were worrying some people around this time
in Britain and America. In America the *Nation* expressed
concern about the increasing power of the press and in
Britain in 1870 the monthly *Cornhill Magazine* had suggested
that Parliament had 'now become merely a body for register-
ing the edicts of our supreme rulers – the newspapers'. The
press was beginning to set the news and political agenda
in ways which many commentators in both Britain and the
States found highly disturbing.

But there is another irony in Stanley's marching the *New
York Herald* expedition into Ujiji under the Stars and Stripes.
For the *Herald* had – notoriously – not been able to lay its
hands on the Union flag ten years before, at the start of the
Civil War. A furious mob had surrounded their Manhattan
offices in April 1861, demanding that the newspaper display
the Stars and Stripes from its windows in support of the
Northern Union. Eventually an office boy had to be sent out
to buy a Union flag. The *New York Tribune* reported mali-
ciously that the *Herald* office was, however, well stocked with
Confederate flags, and it is true that 'The New York *Herald*
had long been seen as the Northern champion of the South',
pro-slavery and contemptuous of 'abolition clamours' and
'Negro mania', and the paper opposed Civil War for as long
as possible, representing it as a cynical and artificial crisis
created by incompetent politicians and abolitionist 'extrem-
ists'. One of its two chief rivals, the *New York Times*, complained: 'Is there to be no end to the *Herald*'s open advocacy
of treason and rebellion? That print has … done everything
in its power to incite the South to the open war into which
they have now plunged the country.' It is clear that the *Times*

feared that the *Herald* wielded considerable power over the people. The *Herald*'s founder and editor, James Gordon Bennett Sr, fulminated against the war in his editorials, a war he described as 'the Anglo-Saxon race destroying itself'. This echoed Stanley's view that the North fought to save the Union and not to free slaves. The *Herald* was more or less forced to get behind the Union once the war had started, but it never became a 'party' paper and continued its iconoclastic tactics in its political reporting. It would always claim to be the newspaper of the people, rather than of the politicians, and in this sense it was, even in the 1840s, strikingly 'modern', especially if compared to the British broadsheets at this time with their partisan and formal reporting.

James Gordon Bennett Sr certainly saw the newspaper as the successor to the book, the theatre and the Church in its influence on public opinion, declaring in 1835 in the first issue of the *Herald*, 'A newspaper can send more souls to Heaven, and send more to Hell, than all the churches or chapels in New York – besides making money at the same time.'

It is difficult to overestimate the importance of the *New York Herald* in America and Europe in the mid-nineteenth century. It had the highest circulation figures of any newspaper in the world. One of the keys to its wide European readership was in its innovation of up-to-date daily financial and business news from Wall Street. Bennett established a European Bureau in 1838. He also pioneered a new 'popular' and sensational form of journalism – running the very first 'interview' in a newspaper in 1836, characteristically with the madame of a brothel in which a prostitute had been murdered. He launched the 'human interest' story, and if Bennett did suggest to Stanley that he might find Livingstone, it was for 'human interest' and not from any high-minded political motive: '[I]t was not the news he cared so much about, as the grand fact of Livingstone's being alive or dead,' remembered Stanley. But, while contemporary critics in America and – even more so – in Britain wrung their hands at the decline of culture which the *Herald* seemed to represent, it might be argued that this was not a decline so much as a seismic shift in the culture. Far from being 'emptied out' of political significance, Bennett's new style of 'human interest' stories could be said to have re-engaged the public, through sentiment and feeling, with political issues that had formerly remained the domain of 'high politics'. In an era of mass publishing and consumption, the presentation of politics was bound to change. The Livingstone and Stanley meeting is one of the first international 'celebrity' moments in history. The hugely wide diffusion of the story and the pictures across Europe and America probably did more to raise public awareness of racial and imperial issues and of the slave trade in Africa than any number of editorials in the London *Times* or Horace Greeley's quality anti-slavery newspaper, the *New York Tribune*. When Stanley's Livingstone story hit the headlines in 1872, it represented a new form of political communication, and was the harbinger of a new kind of public sphere that would develop through the last third of the century.

Despite his own enthusiastic popularisation and sentimentalisation of political issues, Charles Dickens was troubled by the cheap American newspaper press and had satirised Bennett's 'perfect understanding of the public sentiment' in his novel *Martin Chuzzlewit* (1841), in which a newsboy advertises the paper's 'exclusive account of a flagrant act of dishonesty committed by the Secretary of State when he was eight years old; now communicated, at great expense, by his own nurse'. The paper's power also had something to do with the fact that by 1850 89 per cent of white Americans in the North were literate. That was 17.4 million readers. If we compare this to 60 per cent in the UK at the same date, which represented 12.6 million, the comparative size and reach of the newspaper market in the States is immediately obvious. But the market was also a qualitatively different one – far more ordinary working people read a paper every day in America than in England. As one American commentator put it, 'The newspaper seems to be an institution specially calculated to advance in this country. Everybody reads it.' The Civil War only increased the power of the press and helped to make Americans aware of one another across the country in a way that they had not been before. In *Martin Chuzzlewit* Dickens mischievously names American newspapers the *Sewer*, the *Stabber*, the *Family Spy*, the *Private Listener*, the *Peeper*, the *Keyhole Reporter* and the *Rowdy Journal*, and elsewhere describes them as 'so filthy and so bestial that no honest man would admit one into his house, for a water-closet door-mat'. The violation of privacy that Dickens identifies with the American press is a comment on Bennett's development of 'human interest' stories, but it also bespeaks Dickens's more general worry about American 'democracy'. The British national character, he seems to imply, respects boundaries; the American does not. According to Dickens, American newspapers insinuate themselves everywhere and are read everywhere. It would not have surprised him, although he was dead by the time it hit the news in 1872, that the *Herald* had sent Stanley to winkle out Livingstone and to expose him to the glaring light of global publicity.

The war had also made *news* the main content of newspapers, whereas formerly it had been editorial comment
and a more leisured assessment of the facts. Now news was
valuable for its newness. Between newspapers, one contemporary journalist observed, 'The news is the point of rivalry.
The power and success of a newspaper depend wholly and
absolutely on its success in getting and its skill in exhibiting
the news.' Faster rotary presses came into use for newspaper
production in the late 1860s and the *Herald* was very early in
the field when telegraph technology began to speed up the
process of news collection and communication. 'Using the
Atlantic cable and the Russian telegraph, these correspond-
ents ... will send us every item of our intelligence throughout the world, so that we shall place before the reader in
every morning's *Herald* a complete photograph of the world
of the previous day,' boasted Bennett in 1865. By 1866, when
the Atlantic cable first became fully operational, Bennett was
spending more money than anyone else on telegraph news.
In 1866 he famously had a long speech given by the King
of Prussia telegraphed to New York and reported in full, at
a cost of $7,000. This was partly gamesmanship, however.
He wanted to break the Press Association syndicate, which
dictated that all telegraph news had to be shared between
newspapers and they should also share the cost. He therefore started using telegraphs so expensive that no other
paper could afford to follow him – an aggressively competi-
tive tactic typical of the way in which he ran the *Herald* – and
thus he got what he wanted: exclusive telegraph news.

So although Stanley marched into Ujiji with the Stars and
Stripes fluttering in the wind, the *Herald* itself was not a conventional Northern paper: even after the war, it remained
highly racist and staunchly anti-British. Livingstone was to

write to James Gordon Bennett Jr (whose father died in June 1872), asking for his help in the struggle against the slave trade in Africa, 'Now that you have done with domestic slavery forever, lend us your powerful aid towards this great object.' In fact, the issue of slavery would be somewhat buried in the *Herald*'s reports, which concentrated primarily on its own success in beating the British to finding Livingstone and on Livingstone's iconic status, which it simultaneously 'reported' and created. Of course, Livingstone's sympathies in the American Civil War were and always had been with the anti-slavery Unionists in the North – his abhorrence of slavery made this inevitable – and his eldest son had died for the Union cause. The American edition of Livingstone's book *Missionary Travels* had been published by Harper & Brothers, who were well known to be militant Unionists. Livingstone was anxious to hear from Stanley what had developed in America since the end of the war, the impact of which had reached as far as Africa. In 1867 Edward Young had noticed that 'the outer ring of misery caused by the American war had extended here. Calico had been at such a fabulous price, little or none evidently had found its way into the country in exchange for ivory and slaves.' One wonders how much Stanley revealed of his own attitudes and his part in the Civil War in bringing Livingstone up to date. In a 1997 American TV film version of the meeting, *Forbidden Territory: Stanley's Search for Livingstone*, Livingstone assumes Stanley enlisted for the Blues, until Stanley confesses emotionally that he started by fighting for the Confederacy. We do not know what really passed between the two men on this subject. While he was jubilant about the victory of the North and the abolition of slavery, Livingstone was not naïve about the problems now facing America. In a letter to his son Tom in 1869, he had written, 'War brought freedom to 4,000,000 of the most helpless and hopeless slaves ... War has elevated and purified the Yankees and now they have the gigantic task laid at their doors to elevate and purify 4,000,000 slaves.' He added, 'The day for Africa is yet to come.'

In fact, Livingstone's opinion of Americans had not always been very high: 'Aye, they have a great population, viz. 21 millions of the greatest bores the moon ever saw,' he wrote to his parents in 1852, and his opinion of the *New York Herald* was not much better. 'Oh, who has not heard of that despicable newspaper!' he exclaimed on hearing who Stanley's paymasters were. His experience of the Atlantic slave trade had made him – at best – ambivalent about America, and he probably shared in the conventional British anti-Americanism of his time. In 1859 the freed black slave Frederick Douglass had visited Britain from America and found 'American prejudice on the streets of Liverpool and in nearly all ... commercial towns', for example. But Livingstone was genuinely very grateful to Stanley, and to Bennett, who 'at an expense of £4000', as he carefully recorded, had sent the expedition to find him: 'The kindness was extreme and made my whole frame thrill with excitement and gratitude.' Before the Civil War, he had written in *Missionary Travels*:

> The mind naturally turns to the probable influence [the opening up of the new country] may have on Negro slavery; and more especially on the practice of it by a large portion of our own race. We now demand increased supplies of cotton and sugar, then reprobate the means our American brethren adopt to supply our wants. We claim a right to speak about this evil, and also to act in reference to its removal, the more especially because we

are of one blood. It is on the Anglo-American race that the hopes of the world for liberty and progress rest. Now it is very grievous to find one portion of this race practising the gigantic evil, and the other aiding, by increased demands for the produce of slave-labour, in perpetuating the enormous wrong.

Livingstone saw the British as just as culpable in their ever-increasing demand for 'cotton and sugar'. He was slowly to change his tune about America in the course of Stanley's visit, as he saw how the recently victorious Union might prove helpful in supporting his anti-slavery cause.

LIVINGSTONE'S 'CHARACTER'

Towards the end of his life, Stanley wrote that when he was commissioned to find Livingstone he had 'no very fixed idea as to what manner of man he was' and he remembered that 'privately men whispered strange things of him. One, that he had married an African princess, and was comfortably domiciled in Africa; another, that he was something of a misanthrope.' Obviously, for a people that largely considered itself to be racially superior to black Africans, the fear of miscegenation, or of 'going native', was in reality a fear about the fragility of western civilization itself. Part of Stanley's task when he arrived at Ujiji was going to be to assess how far Livingstone had 'gone native' and how far he still belonged to his own culture.

The morning after he marched into Ujiji, Stanley awoke in 'a primitive four-poster, with the leaves of the palm-tree spread upon it' and asked himself where he was, 'What was I sent for? – To find Livingstone. – Have you found him?

– Yes, of course, am I not in his house? Whose compass is that hanging on a peg there? Whose clothes, whose boots, are those? Who reads those newspapers, those 'Saturday Reviews' and numbers of 'Punch' lying on the floor?' Stanley is careful to record that he has discovered Livingstone not a naked savage, but clothed and booted: a reader of newspapers and practitioner of modern science. The American film *Forbidden Territory* dramatises Stanley's stay with Livingstone as a kind of conversion experience. It is true that Stanley's dispatches back from Africa were full of hagiographic descriptions of Livingstone, as Stanley claims that before he met the great man, he 'was only an object to me – a great item for a daily newspaper', but then 'never had I been called to record anything that moved me so much as this man's woes and sufferings, his privations and disappointments, which were now poured into my ear'. '[T]he Hero-traveller and Christian gentleman, LIVINGSTONE' soon won his 'unqualified admiration'. Partly, of course, Stanley wanted to make as much significance and capital out of the story as he possibly could, but it would be unfair to assume that none of this hero-worship was genuine.

Stanley is careful to represent Livingstone as self-sufficient and impervious to the dangerous influences of Africa: '[W]herever he might be, or by whatsoever he was surrounded, his own world always possessed more attractions to his cultured mind than were yielded by external circumstances.' The boundary between the interior space of the ordered Anglo-Saxon mind and body, and the outward environment, figured as impure and uncivilised, is an important one to nineteenth-century Victorian imperialist thinking. Samuel Smiles had already included Livingstone in his best-selling *Self-Help* as an example of a hero '[f]rom the weaver

class', remarking, 'It may be of comparatively little consequence how a man is governed from without, whilst everything depends upon how he governs himself from within.'
The currency of Stanley's newspaper story would depend
upon how far he was able to resurrect Livingstone as a
hero after the disasters of the Universities' Mission and the
mission to Kololo, and in addition he needed to fashion him
into a hero who would be interesting to the American public
as well as to the British. He went about doing this by tapping
into one of the favourite ideas of the day – that of the Anglo-
Saxon character.

ANGLO-SAXONS

Stanley stayed with Livingstone for much longer than he
had planned. Instead of hurrying back to the coast with
his exclusive scoop, he stayed for five months, and on 27
December 1871 Stanley and Livingstone set off on a little
expedition of their own around Lake Tanganyika. This gave
Stanley another opportunity to hoist the Stars and Stripes:

> The canoes – great lumbering hollow trees – are laden
> with good things; the rowers are in their places; the flag
> of England is hoisted at the stern of the Doctor's canoe;
> the flag of America waves and rustles joyously above
> mine; and I cannot look at them without feeling a certain
> pride that the two Anglo-Saxon nations are represented
> this day on this great inland sea, in the face of wild nature
> and barbarism.

The Union Jack and the flag of America joyously fluttering together represent 'the two Anglo-Saxon nations …

9. *The Stars and Stripes and the Union Jack flutter over Stanley and Livingstone's canoes as they set out on their joint exploration of Lake Tanganyika.*

in the face of wild nature and barbarism'. Anglo-Saxonism was enjoying an enthusiastic revival in Britain and America in the mid-nineteenth century, and it had reached a peak of popularity in Britain in the late 1860s. In a bid to differentiate British democratic freedom and civilisation from what was seen as continental despotism, the British turned to a semi-mythical Anglo-Saxon history to create a racial genealogy that separated them from their revolutionary continental neighbours. Rejecting the 'Norman yoke' and disavowing the French influence in British history, they embraced 'Teutonism' instead and created new myths about the foundation of true democracy by the Saxons. In Britain it was felt that America's civil war represented a failure of American democracy, but the years after 1870 saw the slow beginnings of a rapprochement between the two nations and marked the inception of the Anglo-American alliance that is intact today. By 1878 the American *Appleton's Journal* was reporting the Dean describing London's Westminster Abbey as 'the peculiar home of the entire Anglo-Saxon race, on the other side of the Atlantic no less than on this'. When Tony Blair declared on 12 September 2001 that he would stand 'shoulder to shoulder' with George Bush against fundamentalist Islamic despotism and barbarism, it was to the values of Anglo-American Christian democracy that he appealed. Now, as then, the alliance is an uneasy one between two countries fundamentally different in so many ways, but it is still through the symbolism of brotherhood and high-minded sacrifice that it is perpetuated in political rhetoric.

Stanley often describes himself in Africa as 'the Anglo-Saxon', and of Livingstone he wrote, 'His is the Spartan heroism, the inflexibility of the Roman, the enduring resolution of the Anglo-Saxon – never to relinquish his work, though his heart yearns for home; never to surrender his obligations until he can write FINIS to his work.' It is typical of Stanley to group Spartans, Romans and Anglo-Saxons together into a veritable *smorgasbord* of heroic racial characteristics, but, of course, Stanley had his own particular reasons for wanting to avoid emphasising the national differences between 'British' and 'American'. He himself was somewhere in the middle – travelling on an American passport, but in fact born and educated in Wales. 'Anglo-Saxon' conveniently covered all possibilities. He also seems genuinely to have admired Livingstone and wanted to claim kinship with him without having to reveal his own parentage, calling upon the older man to treat him 'as if I were flesh of your flesh, bone of your bone'. Perhaps Stanley was mindful, too, of the expediency of stressing Livingstone's Anglo-Saxon rather than his 'British' qualities when presenting the explorer to the Anglophobic readership of the *Herald*. He repeatedly emphasises the racial brotherhood between the Americans and the British in his descriptions of Livingstone: 'His consistent energy is native to him and to his race. He is a very fine example of the perseverance, doggedness, and tenacity which characterise the Anglo-Saxon spirit.' While the *Herald* would stress Livingstone's British nationality when celebrating its triumph over the British relief expedition, Stanley stressed his Anglo-Saxon race when he wanted to engage his readers with Livingstone's heroism and wisdom.

Stanley reports that Livingstone was a keen Anglo-Saxonist too: 'Neither does he mind my nationality; for "here," said he, "Americans and Englishmen are the same people. We speak the same language and have the same ideas." Just so, Doctor, I agree with you. Here, at least, Americans and Englishmen shall be brothers.' Of course, it was harder for Stanley to keep up this 'Anglo-Saxon' cover when he got back to Europe, as we shall see. Identity – and perhaps particularly national identity – must always be contextual, which meant that when in Africa among what Stanley called 'Ethiop's dusky children' (by which he means black African people of all ages), Stanley and Livingstone were both 'Anglo-Saxons', but when in Britain Stanley was American or possibly Welsh, but either way emphatically not English, and not 'one of us'.

It was 'here' in Africa and not 'there' that Americans and British were able to be 'brothers', but Stanley does also draw our attention to the enormous rifts between the two nations in the early 1870s. 'I see that the Arabs are wondering that you, an Englishman, and I, an American, understand each other. We must take care not to tell them that the English and Americans have fought, and that there are "Alabama" claims left unsettled, and that we have such people as Fenians in America, who hate you.' The Alabama claims were the American claims for compensation from the British government for pro-South activities during the Civil War, despite an official declaration of neutrality. Confederate ships had been built and had sailed from British ports, the *Alabama* among them, and had done immense damage to the Federal fleet. The claims were not settled for seven years after the end of the war, until the summer of 1872 – the same summer that Stanley's Livingstone scoop hit the news. Until then, historians remind us that '[r]elations between the two countries were gravely strained' and Anglophobia was seen as an essential component of American patriotism. Stanley's handshake with Livingstone was timely, reported as it was alongside the successful settlement of the claims that same summer.

The *New York Methodist* in July 1872 reported, 'The English dailies are quite enthusiastic over this American achievement, and the stock expressions about "one blood" and "one kindred" are gone over again with great heartiness.' In British newspaper reports of the meeting, Anglo-Saxonism was used to detract attention from the American triumph in finding Livingstone (and the concomitant British failure), but the *Herald* was having none of this. As far as Bennett was concerned, Stanley was an American, through and through, and his story represented 'a splendid triumph of the whole American press'. Banner headlines had not yet come into use in 1872, but one column header in the *Herald* made the point even more explicitly: 'A feeling of Shame Mingled with Joy at the Herald's Triumph. The Work of England left to a foreign newspaper.'

STANLEY'S PARTING FROM LIVINGSTONE

In Scotland, in the Blantyre David Livingstone Centre, a panel that represents Stanley's parting from Livingstone is puzzlingly entitled 'Renunciation'. It is presumably Livingstone who is renouncing the road back to Europe with Stanley, although maybe it is Stanley's renunciation of Livingstone as he writes emotionally about his parting from the man who had nursed him through another attack of fever with 'very tender and fatherly kindness'. He figures himself as surprised by this; having distrusted Livingstone as an 'Englishman', he had 'intended to interview him, report in detail what he said, picture his life and his figure, then bow him my "*au revoir*", and march back'.

On 1 July 1872 the *Herald* was still assuming that Stanley would be marching back with Livingstone, as 'it is hardly probable that he would diverge one step from the direct road to his native country and to his expectant friends and admirers'. But Livingstone did not in fact leave Africa. Stanley reports that he claimed, ' "I would like very much to go home and see my children once again, but I cannot bring my heart to abandon the task I have undertaken."' It is not quite clear what exactly that task was, but it is true that Livingstone had become increasingly obsessed with finding the source of the Nile, and had developed a morbid fear that, without another heroic 'discovery' to his name, he would be forgotten and would return to a life of penury in Britain. He wrote to his daughter Agnes, 'To return unsuccessful would mean going abroad to an unhealthy consulate to which no public sympathy would ever be drawn.' Although he could have had no idea of how extreme would be the media reaction to Stanley's story, Livingstone must have realised that it would be perfectly possible to travel back with the journalist, and that in so doing he could have ensured that his description of the massacre at Nyangwe and of the hideous practices associated with the slave trade would get a proper hearing back in Britain and in America. But it seems that he did not really want to leave without winning his game. Livingstone's heroism was also a kind of stubbornness. He confided to William Cotton Oswell, 'I don't like to leave my work so that another may "cut me out" and say he has found sources south of mine.' Stanley, on the other hand, was definitely ready to go. He had appreciated the good things he had experienced with Livingstone, but Africa would not hold him, for '[t]here was fever; there were no books, no newspapers, no wife of my own race and blood, no theatres, no hotels, no restaurants, no East River oysters, no mince-pies, neither buckwheat cakes'. Livingstone accompanied him a little of the way on his journey and then the two 'Anglo-Saxons' parted, Stanley apparently in tears: 'We wrung each other's hands, and I had to tear myself away before I unmanned myself; but Susi, and Chumah, and Hamoydah – the Doctor's faithful fellows – they must all shake and kiss my hands before I could quite turn away. I betrayed myself!' Writing about it in the summer of 1872, Stanley says, 'Already it all appears like a strange dream.' As with the meeting, the parting is often figured as two men taking their leave of one another in a wilderness – in the Blantyre panel Stanley and Livingstone stand a little apart from the black Africans, who are bearing large bundles. But in fact Susi, Chuma and Hamoydah participated fully in the farewell.

STANLEY'S SCOOP

Word was certainly out in London about what Stanley's

expedition was really doing in Africa by the early autumn of 1871 – '[a] Party of Americans is hurrying into the interior with the object of rescuing the doctor from his perilous position' – and the London rumour was reported by the *Herald*. Stanley's first dispatch was published in the *Herald* on 22 December 1871. Thereafter the paper ran general features on Africa and African exploration to keep its readers' appetites whetted, and it sent another 'special' to find Sir Samuel Baker in the Sudan. People were interested, therefore, in the story before it became a story. In 1871, for example, American journalist Richard Grant White started his satirical book *The Fall of Man; or, The Loves of the Gorillas, By a Learned Gorilla*:

One morning in the spring of the present year I … found myself in a forest of Western Africa. I was neither searching for the source of anything nor hoping to meet anybody. But, as I walked on my lonely way, I did soon come upon a man, much be-tattered and bronzed, who was plainly an Anglo-Saxon. He was bathing his feet in a muddy little spring, from which a tiny rill ran out and lost itself in the leafy gloom. As I passed him I turned my head inquiringly, and he looked up and said, 'Yes, my name is Livingstone, and this is it. It empties into a duck-pond about a mile off, and that empties into a series of mill-ponds, each a little larger than the other, from the last of which a river runs into Lake Nyanza. This is it; and so I thought that, as I am rather tired with my tramp, I would bathe my feet. Throw a chip in here, and it will float past Thebes and the Pyramids into the Mediterranean. Just send word to Murchison [Sir Roderick Murchison, President of the RGS, 1851–3] please, that I'll be along presently. Good morning.' 'All right,' I answered; 'good morning,' and continued my walk, thinking how nice and jolly it was to find Livingstone making a wash-pot of the source of the Nile.

Clearly, the object of Stanley's quest was already commonly known in America by the end of 1871. Early in April 1872 the first unconfirmed reports reached Zanzibar of the meeting at Ujiji. By the end of April, Stanley's advance messengers confirmed it all, and on 2 May 1872 the *Herald* ran the column-head 'Livingstone Safe', and the first news also reached London. In May, when Stanley's boat pulled into the harbour at Zanzibar from Bagamoyo, 'the American colours were soon visible, proudly flying from the gaff. The beach was lined with people, native and white, who testified their delight by an unceasing discharge of small arms.' At Zanzibar, Stanley stayed at the American Consulate with the Webb family and recovered some of his strength. He gave a personal letter and a large brown dog to Captain Russell of an American trade ship for him to take to Bennett in New York. The letter was dated 18 May 1872. On 29 May Stanley took a steamer to the Seychelles, but was unlucky in missing the monthly French mail boat by just twelve hours and so had to wait another month before setting sail. He and his party rented a house, which they called Livingstone Cottage. At Aden there was a cable awaiting him from Bennett: 'You are now as famous as Livingstone, having discovered the discoverer. Accept my thanks and the whole world's.' Stanley paid off his boy, Selim Heshmy, once he got to Suez. The *Herald* published a dispatch of 7,000 words from Stanley on 2 July. Having bagged the exclusive scoop, the *Herald* summary was distributed on 3 July to any London paper that wanted it, free of charge, thus ensuring that the story spread rapidly across Europe. Stanley arrived in Marseilles on 24 July and was interviewed by the *Daily Telegraph* correspondent John le Sage. He was scathing about the British Consul at Zanzibar, John Kirk, whom he accused of dragging his heels and not trying hard enough to relieve Livingstone. The interview was published in the *Telegraph* on 25 and 26 July. Bennett was annoyed and immediately cabled 'Stop Talking'. Bennett also footed a bill for £2,000 to telegraph Livingstone's letters in full to his family and friends in Britain from Marseilles. Stanley then caught the express train to Paris, where he was welcomed as a returning hero, but he did not 'stop talking' and spoke against Kirk again. He crossed the Channel and arrived in London at the beginning of August.

THE *NEW YORK HERALD* REPORTS THE MEETING

Livingstone was already pretty well known in America. According to Stanley, 'Americans felt as great an interest in Dr Livingstone as Englishmen did.' On Monday 1 July 1872 two big news items appeared on the front page of the *New York Herald*. A 'scanty and ambiguous' telegraph message about Stanley's success had reached New York from Bombay: 'DR LIVINGSTONE The Herald Correspondent's Meeting with Livingstone at Ujiji – Stanley in Advance of the great Traveller Hurrying on to the Coast.' The other item was the Washington Treaty and the final settlement of the Alabama claims. The anti-British *Herald* gave this story a lot of space over the summer of 1872, and it often bumped up against the story of Stanley and Livingstone, as both news items unrolled on the same pages. On Monday 26 August 1872, for example, two columns next to each other were headed

GENEVA and LIVINGSTONE. 'Geneva' referred to the arbitration process for the Alabama and other claims under the Treaty of Washington, and the *Herald*'s subheading runs, 'England, not America, On Trial'. In the British press, on the other hand, the American question was kept fairly quiet. On 17 August 1872 the *Illustrated London News* reported the Foreign Secretary Lord Granville's speech on the occasion of the summer recess of Parliament: 'It was natural and proper that the conservation of the Treaty of Washington should receive the post of honour ... thanks have been publicly tendered to the Leader of the Opposition for his having been vigilant but silent on the American question.' The episode was neither honourable nor heroic for Britain.

On Tuesday 2 July 1872 the Stanley and Livingstone story really began to break and the *Herald* pulled out the stops in displaying its success.

The following special despatch has been received from the Herald correspondent in London:

London, July 1st, 1872
THE GLORIOUS NEWS
It is with the deepest emotions of pride and pleasure that I announce the arrival this day of letters from Mr Stanley, Chief of the HERALD Exploring Expedition to Central Africa. I have forwarded the letters by mail
... A HISTORIC MEETING
Preserving a calmness of exterior before the Arabs which was hard to simulate as he reached the group,
Mr Stanley said:–
'Doctor Livingstone, I presume?'
A smile lit up the features of the hale white man as he

answered:–
'YES, THAT IS MY NAME.'

The *Herald* was not an illustrated paper, but on 2 July page 3 of the paper was dominated by a massive map of equatorial Africa with capitalised headers running down the side:

LIVINGSTONE

HERALD SPECIAL FROM CENTRAL AFRICA

FINDING THE GREAT EXPLORER

EXCITING HISTORY OF THE SUCCESSFUL HERALD
    EXPEDITION

PERILS AND LOSSES BY SICKNESS, HOSTILE TRIBES AND
    JUNGLE DISASTER

ARRIVAL AT UNYANYEMBE – A REIGN OF TERROR

MIRANBO [SIC] – KING OF UJOWA

THE HERALD CARRIES THE WAR INTO AFRICA

ALLIANCE WITH THE ARABS

TWO VILLAGES CAPTURED – THE NATIVES KILLED – THE
    HERALD COMMANDER FEVER-STRICKEN

AN AMBUSCADE BY MIRAMBO – SLAUGHTER AND FLIGHT
    OF THE ARABS

RALLYING UNDER THE HERALD LEADER AND THE
    AMERICAN FLAG

FORWARD TO UJIJI

A FURTHER JOURNEY OF FOUR HUNDERD MILES

IN SIGHT OF TANGANYIKA LAKE

A TRIUMPHAL ENTRY TO UJIJI – DRUMS BEATING AND
    COLOURS FLYING

THE MEETING WITH LIVINGSTONE

A PICTURE FOR HISTORY – THE GRASP OF THE TWO
    EXPLORERS

EXPLORATIONS BY DR LIVINGSTONE

THE CHAMBEZI THE TRUE SOURCE OF THE NILE

IT IS NOT SUPPLIED FROM TANGANYIKA

THE GREAT DOCTOR TO REMAIN TWO YEARS LONGER

As is clear, Livingstone's anti-slavery mission was not high – or indeed anywhere – on this list of derring-do. The next day, 3 July, the *Herald*, always 'a regular beater of the Anglophobic drum', gleefully informed its readers that a telegram had arrived from London reporting that all the British papers were full of its triumph.

Over the following weeks, the *Herald* excerpted and reprinted reports from other newspapers and journals – British and American – about its Livingstone scoop. It was a newspaper that enjoyed reporting itself as 'the news', and Bennett was presumably determined to get his money's worth after such an enormous expenditure and to keep the story running for as long as possible. Indeed, he managed to eke it out for a whole year. One exasperated reader wrote in asking, 'Can't you "let up" a little on Livingstone? Has he relatives "on" the HERALD that expect to become his heirs?' Many of the quoted excerpts were on the American triumph over the British, often congratulating their readers on their American republicanism in contrast to the rusty and slow monarchy of the 'old world'. For example, the *Globe* was reported as saying, 'It may be admitted that, with thankfulness at the discovery, there may mingle some feeling of shame that the care of one who represented so well the enterprise of England should be left to the newspaper correspondent of a foreign journal.' And the *New York Standard* was reported as remarking of the *Herald* expedition on 3 July, 'In the Old World such an undertaking would only have been fitted out by royalty, but in republican America our leading journals have more power and far greater influence than the head of many monarchies.' The *Boston Advertiser* agreed that 'whatever the result of this novel enterprise may be, it is undeniable that there is something "American" in its conception'. The *Herald* intervened every now and then to congratulate itself once more:

> To have undertaken a project in which the Royal Geographical Society of London, backed by the ready purses of the whole English nation has failed; that the mighty English government had pronounced impossible; for a simple newspaper reporter to carry it out to a successful conclusion, while the government and the Royal Geographical Society and the whole English nation were talking about it, is it not worthy of all praise?

And when the British press was prepared to admit to the 'national humiliation', they were keenly excerpted in the pages of the *Herald* too.

Nationalist triumphalism was definitely the dominant feature of the *Herald*'s reporting of the meeting: 'The natives among the mysterious head waters of ancient Nile have seen the Stars and Stripes, and will not forget them ... The American mode of putting an idea into execution is certainly characteristic, compared with [the British failure to get supplies to Livingstone].' Describing the dinner that the American expatriate community threw for Stanley in Paris on 31 July, the *Herald* gave pride of place to Mr Washburne's speech: 'But the flag still highest in air was the starry banner of our own Republic – (long continued cheering) – that emblem of our nation's glory and grandeur, respected and honoured everywhere by Christian civilization, and saluted with reverence even in the wilds of Africa. (Great applause).'

It was only in late August that the *Herald* paused in its celebration of itself and of America and turned its attention briefly to Africa, and to the question of the African slave trade. It ran an article on Cuba – where African slaves were still being imported, placed next to a feature on 'The *Herald* Livingstone Letters and the Slave Trade'. But the main impetus seems to have come from the British press rather than from Bennett himself. Even early in the month, some British newspapers had already harnessed Livingstone's sudden celebrity to the parliamentary campaign to put an end to the East Africa slave trade. The *Herald* reported, '"The East African Slave Trade" Voice of the English Press on Queen Victoria's Speech regarding the Suppression of the Slave Trade on the Eastern Coast of Africa', placing this next to a column headed 'Dr Livingstone', which in turn abutted the column-head, 'Has England Observed with Due diligence her Treaty Obligations to the United States?' on the settlement of the Alabama claims. The political confusion here is clear: Britain was being pursued by America for settlement for the support of the pro-slavery side in the Civil War, while simultaneously being reported as the enemy of the slave trade. Bennett did attempt to launch a worldwide campaign against slavery and donated $1,000 himself, but the campaign did not excite his readers – perhaps unsurprisingly, given the *Herald*'s known racism as a paper – and he quietly dropped it. His business instinct was excellent: if something failed to kindle the imagination of his public, he let it go immediately. But Bennett's omnipotence was to be tried by the Stanley–Livingstone story. Although he and the *Herald* received much of the praise and congratulation to start with – the *Illustrated London News* and many other illustrated journals published portraits of Bennett in August 1872, for example – he had perhaps underestimated Stanley's talent for self-advertisement and hunger for recognition. Soon his 'simple reporter' was getting far more attention than he was and Bennett resented this bitterly. 'There sprang in his bosom a jealousy of Stanley that almost approached the dignity of hatred,' wrote one historian of the *Herald*.

FORGERY AND IMPOSTURE

There was another sensational news item running alongside the Stanley and Livingstone meeting throughout 1872. From May 1871 onwards, two of the longest trials in English legal history would dominate the newspapers. The Tichborne case, which led to both trials, concerned one Roger Charles Tichborne, the son of Sir James and Lady Henrietta Félicité Seymour Tichborne, who was presumed dead when a ship in which he was thought to be sailing sank in 1854. But his mother never gave up hope of his return and when, in 1865, she placed advertisements in Australian newspapers, her 'son' answered: a butcher from Wagga Wagga, Australia, who returned to England with his black servant, Ben Bogle, to claim his title and inheritance in 1866. The rest of the family contested his identity and claimed he was an impostor. He bore little physical resemblance to Roger Tichborne and, oddly, could not speak French, although as a child Roger had lived in France. But his mother swore he was her son and the case become a focus of class tension in Britain, as many working-class people came to believe that the claimant was not only genuine but the victim of a conspiracy by the elite. In 1874 the claimant was sentenced to fourteen years in prison. Public demonstrations in his defence ensued. A British film about the case, *The Tichborne Claimant*, was made in 1998.

The Tichborne case is by no means irrelevant to the Stanley and Livingstone story, raising as it did just at that moment questions about authenticity, identity and imposture, as well as about the establishment's reaction to the 'ordinary man'. In June 1872 the British satirical magazine *Punch* summed up 'What is Always Going On' as 'The weather, the Pope, the publicans, strikes, jobs, Ireland, the American Claims, Dr Livingstone, an international something or other, extraordinary decision of one of "the great unpaid", the Claimant …' Indeed, during the Tichborne trial Livingstone was invoked by the claimant's defence as an example of the problem of maintaining a stable identity throughout long absences. When asked why his client could not spell properly, the lawyer replied, 'Did not Dr Livingstone himself say that he had almost forgotten his own language on coming home from his African travels?' And Stanley himself referred to the case when he reports how, upon his return to Zanzibar after finding Livingstone, '[Captain Fraser] jocosely remarked that it was another Tichborne affair. I was so different that identity was almost lost, even during the short period of thirteen months.' Like the claimant, Stanley returned to England with a black servant, Kalulu.

In fact, Stanley's identity was to prove no laughing matter for him. As soon as the story broke, there was a reaction in the American and the British press, questioning the authenticity of the meeting with Livingstone. The *Boston Advertiser* reported the story with the caveat '[if it all turns out to be true]'; a writer calling himself 'Doubting Thomas' in the *Boston Traveller* reported that '"Stanley" has been heard from again, and this time … comes a report of his meeting with Dr Livingstone … it reads a little like a chapter from Munchausen, neither editor nor reader can say how much of it is true or how much false.' The *Brooklyn Times* blamed the *Herald*'s sensational style for the general doubt about the veracity of the scoop:

> Had the HERALD been content to report what Stanley was doing with due regard to *vraisemblance*, it would not have excited suspicion, at least not to any great extent; but when, for sensational purposes, it dressed up its reports in the most outrageous garb, it was natural that people should conclude that the whole thing was, if not absolutely fictitious, a gross exaggeration of facts.

The French newspapers had disbelieved the story at first too. And in Bombay the newspapers debated the claim, publishing 'a considerable amount of correspondence on the discovery of Dr Livingstone'.

In Britain too, as we shall see, many expressed their disbelief in Stanley's story, perhaps fuelled by anti-American feeling, and Livingstone's family was anxiously petitioned for their confirmation that the letters they had received via Stanley were authentic and not forgeries. On 3 August *The Times* printed a letter from Lord Granville, authenticating Livingstone's letters. Tom Livingstone is quoted: 'We have not the slightest reason to doubt that this is my father's journal.' Augusta Fraser remembered 'to my parents' great indignation, doubt was cast on the genuineness of the letters brought home to them from Ujiji by Stanley in 1872'. She mentions Livingstone's affectionate greetings to 'good Bellis', the children's nurse, as proof of their authorship. This was not an unusual anxiety at the time – the Tichborne case was only a high-profile dramatisation of a more general difficulty opened up by a newly globalising culture and increased mobility in the nineteenth century. Emigrants' letters during the nineteenth century would often contain 'tokens' – either small objects or, more commonly, anecdotes that only the writer could know about the recipient, or vice versa (such as 'Ask James if he remembers the incident concerning my hand and the carding machine') in order to guarantee their provenance.

Many thought 'the whole thing was the construction of a *farceur américain*'. The *Herald* enjoyed the controversy: 'The fogs of doubt which becloud and bemuddle the minds of certain careful individuals whose mental grasp is moderate with regard to whether Stanley ever met Livingstone, whether such a being as Stanley ever existed, whether Livingstone is not a myth, and Africa a mere moonland are doomed to a premature dissolution,' it chuckled. Some of the *Herald*'s critics were suspicious of the language used in Livingstone's dispatches. Expressions such as 'twaddle', 'currency' and 'bulbous-below-the-ribs' were considered suspect as 'Americanisms', and Stanley was accused of forging the documents himself. So when the family confirmed the authenticity of Livingstone's personal letters, the *Herald* saw the chance for even more publicity. On 27 August it published a sample of 'LIVINGSTONE'S SIGN MANUAL. Facsimile of Dr David Livingstone's Letter of Thanks to the *New York Herald*,' graphically reproducing Livingstone's actual handwriting in the paper and proclaiming, 'Now, in the face of all this, to proclaim the letters forgeries is to write one self down an ass, or to attribute to Mr Stanley such powers of imitation, imagination and clairvoyance that there is no way of accounting for all his cleverness except through Spiritualism … It would leave the Tichborne case, with its uncertainties, far in the background.' The *Herald* concluded by dancing a little jig of joy that 'even the high and Royal Geographical doubters' in Britain had had to sign a capitulation. The Stanley story resembled the Tichborne case, at one level, as the story of the elite (the Royal Geographical Society) unfairly challenging and bullying the ordinary man. Bennett pushed this angle, making Stanley's scoop – among other things – the emotive story of the ordinary American man overcoming the massed power of the old-world elite. The *New York Herald* was, after all, the people's paper.

On 24 August 1872 a different kind of doubt was aired about Stanley when one of the *Herald*'s rival papers, the *New York Sun*, published revelations by a former travelling companion of Stanley, Lewis Noe, about a Turkish journey with Stanley in 1866, casting doubt on Stanley's character and accusing him of lying about his origins. It concluded that Stanley's purported meeting with Livingstone was 'the most gigantic hoax ever attempted on the credulity of mankind', sparking a fierce exchange of views between the newspapers which some suspected was partly engineered to push up the circulation of both. According to the *New York Evening Mail*, 'Each generously supplies the other with ammunition. Yesterday the *Sun* borrowed the *Herald*'s plates to show that Livingstone's letters were written by Stanley. Today the *Herald* uses the *Sun*'s plates … If the controversy can be kept up with such an economy of materials there is no knowing how long it may last.' The *Herald* countered:

Mr Stanley was employed by the HERALD to report the Abyssinian war for this journal, and the vigor, capability and faithfulness of the man were shown in his furnishing us with the news of the fall of Magdala and death of King Theodorus before anybody else and in time for us to communicate to the British government the success of its own expedition in that distant region. This was Mr Stanley's certificate of character as a journalist to the world. For what happened in his life before that we are not accountable.

But the seeds of suspicion had been sown and Stanley was to come under prolonged scrutiny on both sides of the Atlantic after this. Who exactly was he? Could he be trusted? Was he American after all?

STANLEY'S RECEPTION IN BRITAIN

News started to trickle into the British newspapers about Stanley's success from the beginning of May. On 3 May 1872 *The Times* printed a telegram from Aden saying that 'natives' reported Livingstone 'alive and well at Ujeeji, where he had been joined by another white man – Stanley. No other details.' On 15 May the President of the RGS, Sir Henry Rawlinson, conceded that such reports might be true, but if they were, he announced, 'it would not be that Mr Stanley had relieved Livingstone, but the exact contrary – that Livingstone had relieved Mr Stanley'. Throughout May Rawlinson, still convinced that the RGS expedition would reach Livingstone first, continued to use a sneering tone in describing the American Stanley: '[H]e had been sent out by our Transatlantic cousins, among whom the science of advertising had reached a far higher stage of development than in this benighted country, for the purpose of "interviewing"

Livingstone and communicating intelligence of his whereabouts to the *New York Herald*, one of the most energetic,
as it was the most popular, of the American newspapers.'
On 20 May the *Herald* published its London correspondent's comments on the British press reaction so far: 'From
what appears in the daily papers it would seem to be the
earnest desire of all persons here interested in geographical
science that the recent good news from Zanzibar may prove
not true.' But it was true. On 14 June a telegram confirmed,
'Stanley arrived at Zanzibar, having left Livingstone alive
and well.' And on 3 July, along with every other paper in the
English-speaking world, *The Times* printed the summary distributed by the *Herald*. From here on, the British press was
entirely dependent upon the *Herald* for its reports. It was
not just that an American had won the race; the Americans
now owned the story and they fed it in tantalising bite-sized
pieces to the British. There were still doubters, just as there
were in the States. One letter published in *The Times* on 9
July said Stanley's story was clearly faked as he described
Livingstone's skin as 'fair', whereas when the explorer had
last been seen in England, he was bronzed brown by the
African sun. But on the whole the British press was quick to
accept Stanley's story and *The Times*, in particular, applauded
him and gave him his 'due meed of praise', while roundly
attacking the failure of the British Livingstone Search &
Relief Expedition: 'He sets off and does it while others are
idly talking or slowly planning. Africa is a very wide target,
but Mr Stanley hit the bull's eye at once.'

When Stanley himself arrived in England on 1 August
1872, he met with a very mixed reception. But on the whole,
the press were supportive and congratulatory. The *Graphic*
printed pictures of 'Dr Livingstone and Mr Stanley – Dr

Livingstone's House at Ujiji – [and] Kalulu, Mr Stanley's Native Attendant'. On 3 August the *Illustrated London News* printed a large portrait of Livingstone on its front page. It introduced its report of Stanley's coup thus: 'It comes to us – strange to say – from an American source. What the expedition organised by the Royal Geographical Society failed to accomplish, Mr Stanley, representing nothing more than the energy and the pecuniary credit of the *New York Herald*, has had the good fortune to compass single-handed.' The article continued, 'We advisedly refrain from discussing the question as to why supplies forwarded to Dr Livingstone from this country did not reach him until after Mr Stanley's successful enterprise, and as to the somewhat humiliating failure of the recently-organised expedition under the auspices of the Royal Geographical Society for the discovery and relief of the great African traveller.' The *Daily Telegraph* likewise felt that '[a] serious and honest *amende* is due to Mr Stanley' from the RGS.

But Stanley had been in the country more than a week before the RGS acknowledged his existence in a letter that was reprinted in *The Times*, claiming rather lamely that this was 'the very earliest opportunity at which it was possible to convey our thanks'. *Punch* had fun with this: 'The President of the Royal Geographical Society, who discovered that Livingstone discovered Stanley and not Stanley Livingstone, has at last discovered that Stanley is in England. This is not a bad discovery. It seems, however, only to have been accomplished after a severe effort.' Stanley was, however, invited by the RGS to address the Geographical Section at the British Association for the Advancement of Science at its meeting in Brighton that month. Some 3,000 people turned up to hear him and 'there was a crowded and fashionable audience, amongst whom were the Emperor Napoleon, the Empress Eugénie, and the Prince Imperial'. But this was to be a disaster.

The Alabama claims had finally been settled that very week, so that there was 'no longer any impediment to a perfect concord between two kindred nations', and W. B. Carpenter reflected this diplomatic resolution when he opened the meeting with a gracious speech: '[L]et us glory in the prospect now opening that England and America will co-operate in that national object which, far more than the discovery of the sources of the Nile, our great traveller has set before himself as his true mission, the extinction of the slave trade.' But Stanley misjudged the formal British scientific tone of the meeting and introduced himself as 'a troubadour', which was probably a mistake, and recounted his adventures on the way to finding Livingstone in his usual rollicking *New York Herald* style. This gave the chairman of the session, Francis Galton, the chance to patronise him, saying, 'in a sweet, smooth, bland voice, "We don't want sensational stories, we want facts."' Galton then went on to embarrass Stanley further by questioning him as to his true nationality. At exactly this time, Galton was working on heredity and identity, and he became increasingly obsessed with the rumours about Stanley's identity. As the founding father of eugenics, he was fascinated by the question of whether Stanley was of the right stock to be a gentleman or not. In fact, revelations about Stanley's past were being published in Britain and America by this time. John Camden Hotten wrote to *The Times* in the middle of November to defend his publication of *Mr. Stanley's Early Life*, declaring – truthfully in fact – that 'Mr Stanley was born in Denbigh, and resided in its neighbourhood for the first fifteen years of his life.' Stanley was still denying any such claim and sticking to his American identity, but at the RGS meeting his American manners were taken as 'rough' and vulgar.

A dinner given by the Brighton and Sussex Medical Society the following evening made matters worse. Stanley, asked to reply to a toast to 'The Visitors', talked in 'a grotesque and humorous strain, expressing his surprise that he should be called upon to return thanks where there were visitors present whose eloquence would rival that of Demosthenes, Pericles, or even their own Daniel Webster'. The President of the Society recorded, 'These remarks were made with considerable gesticulation, which, if not intended, was certainly calculated to excite and encourage laughter' – and the audience did, indeed, laugh, 'but I firmly believe with no intention of casting a sneer or offering any disrespect to Mr Stanley. Mr Stanley then hastily left the room, saying that he did not come there to be ridiculed or laughed at.' This reads like a tale of misunderstanding and misprision. Stanley spoke with a strong American accent that would have sounded strange to most of those present, and he – again – probably made a mistake in trying to show off his classical knowledge in such company. But Stanley was ever sensitive to slights, to the extent that he frequently imagined them, and he added this to his growing list of English social atrocities against him. When Stanley visited Livingstone's friends the Webbs of Newstead Abbey (not to be confused with the other Webb family at the American consulate in Zanzibar) in the autumn of 1872, Mrs Webb told him that he was 'a perfect porcupine with all your quills out'. She became fond of him, nevertheless.

Significantly, the Brighton fiasco was reported entirely differently on the other side of the Atlantic in the *Herald*, which chose to extract a very favourable account of Stanley's performance from the London *Daily News*: 'Gifted with great powers of expression, a sonorous voice, no little humor, abundant capacity for retort and holding his own pleasantly and firmly, Mr Stanley's triumphant début this morning before many of the leading geographers of the world furnished a remarkable example of the power of mother-wit and practical experience.' Again there is a charge of class consciousness here – the 'practical' self-made man Stanley has beaten the professional 'armchair geographers' of the RGS to the story. The reporter does concede, however, that 'some of his opinions may be modified by the light scientific geographers may supply', but added, 'Mr Stanley is essentially the man for a platform and a popular assembly.' In fact, when Stanley did give popular lectures in New York later in the year, they were a miserable failure and the series was cancelled halfway through.

Stanley did not help matters in Britain by persisting in his public accusation that the British government had abandoned Livingstone. He was cheered up at the end of August by the gift of a 'beautiful and valuable gold snuff-box set with brilliants' from Queen Victoria herself and an invitation to an audience with her in September in Scotland. He was never to know that Queen Victoria described him privately as 'a determined, ugly, little man – with a strong American twang'. Whatever else was suspicious about Stanley, clearly his 'American' manners inspired the greatest dislike. But once Stanley had been recognised by the Queen, the RGS really had to fall in line. The Society awarded Stanley its gold medal in October 1872 and threw a dinner in his honour that 'lasted till a very late hour.' The rift was somewhat healed, but British snobbery about Stanley would never really abate and Sir Richard Burton, the African traveller, managed to insult both the missionary ('mish') Livingstone and Stanley when he remarked casually that it would be 'rather infra dig. to discover a mish'.

Always an excellent self-publicist, while he was in the UK Stanley spoke at a large public anti-slavery meeting at the Mansion House in London. Livingstone's father-in-law, Robert Moffatt, was also present. Stanley was 'received with loud and prolonged cheers' and 'it was impossible for him to proceed until he had mounted on a chair, in order that he might be seen by the audience in the remoter parts of the room'. Stanley gave an impassioned anti-slavery speech in which he asked the audience to imagine a slave market in the centre of London of the kind that existed in Zanzibar. When his children's book *My Kalulu* was published in 1874, he dedicated it 'to those who have aided in the suppression of slavery on the east coast of Africa'. But his support for the British anti-slavery campaign dwindled and by the mid-1870s he had already moved away from Livingstone's liberal views of African people, reverting to a position nearer the racism he had grown up with in New Orleans and Arkansas.

At precisely the moment that Stanley's scoop was being reported, Blanchard Jerrold was writing about Gustave Doré's famous pictures of life in London in 1872 and noting 'that general enemy known as the "swell"'. The 'swell' song was at its peak in the music halls in the late 1860s and early 1870s, and George Leybourne, music-hall entertainer and 'the original Champagne Charlie', was contracted to act the 'swell' off stage as well as on and to parade around London in a carriage in a fur-collared coat in 1868 and 1869. In 1872 and 1873 there was a wages boom for the British working classes and so Stanley appeared just at a moment when working-class aspirations to better status and commodities had become briefly realisable. Stanley, who was later to parade around America in a specially customised carriage with 'Henry Morton Stanley' emblazoned on the side, could, like Laybourne, be accused of being a vulgar 'swell' – energetic, confident and defiant of authority, a man's man and, to some extent, a fraud. In Stanley many recognised a 'type' – and this partly accounts for the ambivalence of British reactions to him. That he was not quite what he seemed was both reason for congratulation, as he had pluckily managed to pull himself up the social scale, but also for suspicion – who was he, anyway? Horace Waller called on Stanley in London in the summer of 1872, and wrote to Livingstone that he detected Stanley in a lie, and was astonished by Stanley's duplicity: '[W]hen I saw the sang froid with which this man quickly shifted his cigar to other [sic] side of his mouth, and the subject, without a word, to something else, I confess, Doctor, I did feel very sorry for you.' Stanley did not seem quite gentlemanly, for sure.

Stanley left the UK angry at the way in which he had been treated, having written in August 1872 to Livingstone's daughter Agnes about 'the vile insinuations of some portions of the English press'. In a letter to another sympathiser, he wrote:

> first they would sneer at the fact of an American having gone to Central Africa, then they sneered at the idea of him being successful – then when they heard my name they tried to rob me of it – in one paper I was Smith, in another I was Jones, in another Thomas, and now they have changed it to Rowlands ... [A]fter decently burying

Livingstone in forgetfulness they hate to be told he is yet
alive. What a country!

This is a complicated double bluff, of course, as Rowlands
was, in fact, Stanley's real name. Stanley could not believe
that 'people would rather hope that Dr Livingstone would
be irrecoverably lost than that an American journalist should
find him'. He felt he had been mocked and laughed at, and
was relieved to return to New York in November 1872, where
he was greeted by a *New York Herald* yacht draped with a
huge banner with WELCOME HOME, STANLEY! emblazoned across it in letters two feet high. The champagne corks
popped all the way into New York harbour. Here, he could
be an unequivocal hero.

JOHN BULL AND UNCLE SAM IN 1872

But in Britain, some of the laughter was in truth tinged with
consternation. The Stars and Stripes appeared again in an
illustration in the British satirical publication *Punch* after
Stanley's news had broken. The sketch shows Livingstone
reclining in a hammock made out of the Stars and Stripes flag
and the 'Private and Confidential' letter from Dr Livingstone
to Dr Punch complains, '[W]hy shouldn't I be allowed to
enjoy myself, and take my own time about it, without being
tracked, and dogged, and hunted for, like a sovereign in a
dust-bin ...?' Especially when the discoverers are 'to pocket
a heap of coin by making capital out of me'. As so often in
Punch, it is not entirely clear who is the butt of the joke here.
Livingstone is pictured cradled in the American flag, but
America is implicitly accused of commercialism and sensationalism in setting out to find him. Reactions to Stanley in

the British press reveal the more general worry that what had until now generally been considered American 'vulgarity' might in fact turn out to be American force and purposefulness. Britain had always depended upon imported American cotton, but had grown to depend more and more on American food imports throughout the economically depressed 1860s. The victory of the North in the Civil War had represented, in Britain, a moral victory for the radical MP John Bright and the British pro-reform radicals, and this had troubled more conservative commentators. In the early 1870s it was becoming less and less easy to dismiss America as an 'uncivilised' and 'empty' country.

The *Herald*'s correspondent in the Sudan, Alvan S. Southworth, wrote of British exploration in Africa:

> it has been conducted too much in the fashion of the British tourist, and too many theodolytes, barometers, sextants and artificial horizons have replaced canned meats and desiccated necessities. I am of the opinion (hastily formed perhaps) that twelve energetic, live, I might say reckless Americans, each with his special mental and physical gifts, could bare this whole continent to the view of an anxious mankind. The British are good, hardy, stubborn travellers, but they are like their journalism and ideas – slower than the wrath of the Grecian gods.

A British newspaper, on the other hand, had characterised America as a nation of 'no repose, no moderation, … We walk, planting one foot firmly before we take another step; they "go ahead" on the slipperiest ground, until they fall.' The stereotypes are obvious, and persist in various ways to this day. In fact, Stanley's 'go ahead' expedition to find

Livingstone had left the British standing. It was an uncom-
fortable reminder that British superiority was no longer so
secure as it had seemed at mid-century. In 1872 Stanley was
seen as standing for everything that was 'go ahead' about
America.

AMERICAN AND BRITISH FILM VERSIONS OF THE MEETING

It is extraordinary how this meeting between a 'pretend'
American and a Scottish 'Englishman' has continued to
focus Anglo-American tensions in its tellings and retellings. The 1925 silent British film *Livingstone* shot over a
full year on location in Africa with the help of the LMS
and Universities' Mission to Central Africa (UMCA), was
the darling project of M. A. Wetherall, who directed, produced *and* starred as Livingstone, delivering a surprisingly poignant performance in the role. The film was very
well received in Britain, where 'the name of Livingstone is
such a household word in so many families'. Its dramatisation of the meeting scene was more or less a *tableau vivant*
from the *Illustrated London News* illustration. The *New York
Times* commented, 'Looking at this film is like turning the
pages of an old picture book', and felt that Wetherall had
not done 'full justice' to the meeting scene. The shot is a
wide one, there are no close-ups and no attempt at inter-
preting the encounter psychologically. Indeed, despite its
sentimental script, the style of the film is so documen-
tary that the makers of Niall Ferguson's *Empire* series on
TV were able to use a sequence from it – in which Stanley
is pictured moving across the African landscape with his
caravan – silently implying that this was 'real' footage of
the expedition. In *Empire* Ferguson deals fairly summarily

10. The meeting between Stanley and Livingstone was filmed on location in Ujiji for the 1925 silent British film Livingstone.

with the meeting: 'It took an American to raise the art of British understatement to its zenith,' he comments, and he interprets the meeting between Stanley and Livingstone as 'a meeting between two generations'. Livingstone's generation believed in the moral rebirth of Africa, Stanley's was a harder-nosed imperialism that wanted Africa for itself. 'Stanley believed only in brute force,' he adds, and says no more about the younger man, perhaps because in this version of the meeting, Stanley remains 'American' and the focus of the *Empire* series was on Britain.

The 1925 film was made in a deliberate attempt to compete with Hollywood. In the 1920s British film production was in decline and, to some anxious observers, American movies seemed to be flooding in, many of them showing Britain and the British in a poor light. Viscount Burnham, the proprietor of the *Daily Telegraph*, predicted that all-British films such as *Livingstone* would prove that the British were not 'mere imitators and followers of the United States'. W. G. Ormsby-Gore, Under-Secretary of State for the Colonies, said the 'ordinary sensational crime film was a most formidable agent for evil' in the British Empire and 'more British films of the type of *Livingstone* were essential as a corrective'. Viscount Burnham even tried to set up the British Empire Film Institute in 1926 to make more films like *Livingstone*, predicting that, without an effort at re-education, 'the younger generation nurtured on these American ideas [will] base their lives on American ideas of morals and American ideas of life generally...[which are] ... alien to all ideas of life and thought in this England of ours'. In 1935 the same arguments were rolled out when the *Geographical Magazine* was founded, a British version of the American *National Geographic* that was established in much the same spirit of emulation yet sniffiness about Americanisation.

Wetherall had in fact hoped to release the film in the United States in 1926, but the New York City distributors refused to take it, arguing that they would be unable to promote it successfully because Livingstone was not well enough known to Americans. James Macnair reported difficulty in fund-raising in America for the Blantyre Livingstone Memorial near Glasgow at around the same time. Clearly, Livingstone was not as much of a 'household name' in the States as he was in Britain in the early twentieth century. By 1929 an American distributor was secured for the film and it played for a week in New York City, but it appears to have sunk without trace after this. The *New York Times* had sighed that 'the direction is sadly unimaginative', and Wetherall's silent film could not compete with the American movie industry, which had brought in 'talkies' in 1927 with *The Jazz Singer.*

Wetherall was to die in 1939, the year that his nightmare came true – the Americans took up the Livingstone story and made a big-budget movie out of it. But this was not a film about Livingstone; as we have already seen, this was an action-adventure film about Stanley, who was played by the Hollywood star Spencer Tracy. In *Stanley and Livingstone*, the British at Zanzibar are seen as well-intentioned but feeble, and, crucially, old. A British expedition funded by the *London Globe* (a fictitious paper, and incident) has recently failed. Stanley, by contrast, is a go-ahead young American working for a 'pushy Yankee mag' who promises Bennett that he will find Livingstone alive or dead, and if dead, 'I'll bring him back in alcohol for Barnum's new museum on 14th Street.' Barnum was P. T. Barnum, the nineteenth-century American showman and circus director. The film plays upon ideas about British snobbery about Americans – Stanley has to point out to the proprietor of the *London Globe*, for example, '[Q]uite a large proportion of Americans read.' The meeting is handled very differently in this film version, as Stanley worries out loud, 'I don't know what to say when you meet people in Africa.' His fictional sidekick, the cowboy Jeff Slocum, suggests, 'Howdy pard, how's tricks?' but Stanley delivers the immortal line when he does encounter Livingstone at last, to the strains of 'Onward Christian Soldiers' on the violin. The two men's faces are shot in close-up to emphasise the deep emotion and solemnity of the moment. The film plays up Livingstone's shock when he discovers that Stanley is the envoy of a newspaper. 'The only reason you were sent here was to get news for your paper,' he says, and Stanley replies, 'When we get through building you up you'll be a

11. *The meeting between Stanley and Livingstone in the 1939 American film* Stanley and Livingstone.

sensation across three continents.' Livingstone slowly educates Stanley into greater sympathy with Africa, by comparing it to America – a 'blank space on the map', just as the first settlers saw the United States. And when Stanley leaves Livingstone, he has likewise brought the Doctor round to the efficacy of the American way. 'This time I know my message will go through,' says Livingstone. In fact, the screenplay was rewritten to make the focus of the film more American. The script originally opened in 1854 with David Livingstone at a parliamentary meeting planning British imperial expansion and then cut to Dickensian scenes of Stanley's early life in the workhouse. In the final version, though, these scenes were removed and the film started instead in the American Wild West, leaving Stanley's British origins to be revealed at the very end. The 1930s and 1940s saw America establishing itself as a global presence, not through imperialism but through technology and communications. The new American cultural imperialism worked through the manipulation of image and spectacle. Stanley – and by association, America – is seen in the film as the protector of Christian civilisation, stepping in under the banner of enterprise rather than of empire. *Stanley and Livingstone* gestures towards the wartime alliance of what the Anglo-American British Prime Minister Winston Churchill was memorably to call the 'English-speaking peoples'.

Back in 1872, the meeting of Stanley and Livingstone in Ujiji offered a useful and timely paradigm of cordial Anglo-American relations after the divisions over slavery and the American Civil War. To some degree, both the British and American press used the meeting as a means of consolidating and legitimating a new identity for America – as a global force for good. Now itself free of slavery, America had a duty to fight against slavery worldwide and in the process to export its democratic, individualist and capitalist values to the 'uncivilised' world.

The phrase 'Dr Livingstone, I presume?' survives today because it carried a direct comic charge in 1872, and it entered the culture immediately on both sides of the Atlantic. In

America it was funny because it showed the Americans getting the better of the British, but also because it tapped into uneasiness about the relationship between Yankee sincerity and Yankee vulgarity in the democracy of post-bellum America. In Britain it was funny because Stanley was not a gentleman and seemed hardly to be trusted. But it also made the British laugh a little anxiously too, at the English gentlemen's dilatoriness in rescuing Livingstone, and the ponderousness of their elite system more generally.

Now, of course, those contemporary ironies have fallen out of the story and the episode has become emptily iconic in a way that Conrad disgustedly remarked upon in 1923. Standing near the spot where Livingstone and Stanley had met fifty years earlier, he recalled 'no great haunting memory, but only the unholy recollection of a prosaic newspaper "stunt"'. Prosaic it may have been, but Stanley's newspaper stunt was also historic in creating a new kind of celebrity which was to play an important role in the development of an emergent form of popular and political culture in the last third of the nineteenth century.

3

'FAITHFUL TO THE END'

For three nights in April 1874 the silent Map Room at the headquarters of the Royal Geographical Society on Savile Row, London, harboured a strange inhabitant. A coffin of English oak, draped in a Union Jack and 'surrounded by palms and arum lilies', rested – solid and intractable – all night long on its trestles. During the day, crowds filed by to pay their respects. Inside was what remained of the body of David Livingstone: his embalmed 'shell', from which his internal organs had been removed and buried by his African servants in a flour tin under a tree in the East African village of Ilala.

Exhausted by travelling, suffering terrible internal bleeding, Livingstone had died in Chitambo's village in Africa in May 1873. His African servants, in an extraordinary act, carried his mummified body over 1,000 miles across Africa to Zanzibar and the coast so that he could be returned to his own people. The arrival of Livingstone's body at Southampton docks on 15 April 1874 and his state funeral and burial at Westminster Abbey on 18 April, at which Stanley was a coffin-bearer, were almost obsessively reported in the media 'amid a general manifestation of public feeling as remarkable as it was impressive'. What was that 'public feeling' all about? State funerals in the nineteenth century were generally only granted to military heroes, prime ministers and royalty, and only a handful took place in Westminster Abbey between William Pitt the Younger's in 1806 and Livingstone's in 1874. Was Livingstone's state funeral primarily a national event or a religious one? Or was there something political in the public demonstrations of grief by the thousands of people who lined the route of the funeral procession?

LIVINGSTONE'S BODY

On 27 January 1874 a telegram was sent from Zanzibar via Aden to the London Foreign Office. It was from Lieutenant Verney Lovett Cameron, who had been sent to find and assist Livingstone in November 1872 by the Royal Geographical Society, which was probably already anxious about losing the explorer again. Cameron had encountered Livingstone's servants returning to the coast, bearing their master's body, and wrote, 'Please telegraph orders as to disposal. No leaden shells procurable here.' By leaden shells, he meant the lead coffin liners that would normally be used when transporting a corpse over a long distance to prevent unwholesome leakages of putrefied matter. In fact, Cameron had done his best to persuade Livingstone's black servants to bury the corpse in Unyanyembe, where he met them, and some accounts suggest that he bullied them, but they stood their ground and insisted that he help them to return the remains of Livingstone to Britain. The body was duly sent from Zanzibar to Aden on board the *Calcutta*, and then from Aden to Suez and back to Britain on the *Malwa*. Mr Arthur Laing, an English merchant from Zanzibar, and Jacob Wainwright, one of Livingstone's black servants, travelled with the body.

Macabre though it may seem, the human remains, already nine months old when they left Africa, arrived in Britain more than eleven months after Livingstone's death. It was just as well, then, that the body was not putrefying in the way that had troubled the British public after the Duke of Wellington's death twenty years before. The Duke's burial had been postponed for two months after he died, and it was necessary to encase the body in four coffins – of pine, English oak, lead (of twice the usual thickness) and mahogany. But Livingstone's 'withered remains', as Sir Samuel Baker referred to them, were reassuringly unbodily, and the newspapers stressed the way in which he had been eviscerated and mummified by his African servants. A telegram forwarded from the *New York Herald* and reprinted in the *Illustrated London News* reported, 'The body was preserved in salt and dried in the sun for twelve days ... the body ... was placed in a coffin formed of bark, then journeyed to Unyanyembe in about six months.' Susi, who had been Livingstone's favourite servant, according to Stanley, had asked Wainwright, who was literate in English, to write out an inventory of all Livingstone's possessions. The process of embalming the body had been lengthy and complicated. The intestines and internal organs had been removed by another servant, Farjullah, who had been a medical doctor's assistant at Zanzibar, with the help of Carus Farrar. Chuma and Susi later remembered that they had noticed 'a large clot of blood about the size of the hand inside about where the liver is on the right side' when they removed the intestines. Wainwright had read the Christian burial service as the tin box containing these innards was lowered into the ground. Susi, Manua Sera and Chuma were all present at the burial. Wainwright carved an inscription on the tree under which the box was buried: DR LIVINGSTONE, MAY 4, 1873. Livingstone also had an African funeral, which was organised by his African servants. The King of Ilala had 'summoned all the chiefs, men and women of his country to come out with their drums and other materials to morn [sic] for the Dr after their custom'. The drumming and dancing went on for two days.

The packing of the open trunk of the body with salt and the drying process took place behind a carefully constructed screen. The face was bathed in brandy, as an extra preservative, and the servants bent the legs of the body back at the knees so as to make a shorter package for carrying. The body was then wrapped in calico and encased in a cylinder of bark before being sewn into a large piece of sailcloth. Finally it was tarred to make it watertight, by the same method that African boats – or dhows – were waterproofed, and they were ready to set off. The head of the village, Chitambo, was left with a biscuit tin and copies of British newspapers as evidence that Livingstone had been there, should anyone come looking for him. At Baula, Jacob Wainwright wrote a letter that was taken to Unyanyembe by Chuma and three colleagues. The Acting Consul at Zanzibar, Captain W. F. Prideaux, sent Chuma back with supplies. When the rest of the party arrived at Unyanyembe the body had to be wrapped in calico and disguised as a bundle of cloth, as Wagogo law in those parts forbade the transportation of human remains. When the Africans finally arrived with the body at Bagamoyo on the coast, they were summarily paid their wages and dismissed by Prideaux, while a warship, disturbingly named HMS *Vulture*, was called to collect the corpse and deliver it to Zanzibar. Later, Horace Waller and others expressed their surprise that the 'faithful' servants Susi and Chuma had not

12. 'Carrying the Body to the Coast': a magic lantern slide from a series of forty images, The Life and Works of David Livingstone *published by the London Missionary Society around 1900.*

been invited to attend Livingstone's British funeral. 'The task that these men performed was truly Herculean,' Waller complained, maintaining that they should have been better rewarded.

This was the same Horace Waller who took over the editing of Livingstone's *Last Journals* when it became clear that Livingstone's son Tom was making a mess of it. Waller carefully expunged all the physical details of Livingstone's death. In the published journals there is no mention of the latrine that his servants had dug for him in the corner of his hut during his illness, or the way in which his dead body had to be covered in tar not just to waterproof it but because it was stinking so badly as it decomposed that the men were unable to eat. Waller suppressed other details too: Cameron's close friend, Dr W. E. Dillon, for example, had committed suicide by shooting himself through the head on the way back to the coast with the expedition accompanying the body, and the detail of Susi collecting scattered fragments of his skull with the help of a little dog are tastefully expunged from the finished edition. Livingstone himself never suppressed such disturbing details: 'A Slave tied to a tree dead & putrid & greatly eaten by the Hyaenas,' he wrote in his journal, and he even drew an accompanying sketch. Indeed, when John Murray was editing *Missionary Travels*, he had had gently to point out to Livingstone that words such as 'urine' would be unacceptable to his British readers. Waller similarly cut out all of Livingstone's frequent disquisitions on his painful haemorrhoids in his journal and changed Livingstone's 'testicles' to 'tenderest parts' and 'bottom' to 'a place where no bones are likely to be broken'. Waller was also the first to enshrine the image of Livingstone's pious death on his knees in prayer. Thus the body, and any suggestion of bodily corruption, were expunged from the memory of Livingstone. By the time it arrived on British soil, nearly a year after his death, Livingstone's body had been purified of all suspicion of material corruption. Blackened and dried out like the saints' bodies preserved in Catholic churches, Livingstone had been both literally and imaginatively transformed from mortal remains to immortal relic. He had become, in Richard Monckton Milnes's words, a 'sacred crust'.

The fact that Livingstone's remains were being returned 'home' posed a problem for his family, who were left in some financial distress at his death. Indeed, in April 1874 a memorial fund was opened, inviting subscriptions for the benefit of his family, and Anna Mary, Agnes and William Oswell Livingstone were each granted Civil List pensions of £50 per year in May. As the explorer's body was wending its slow passage home, the Prime Minister, Disraeli, was caught slightly off guard in the middle of a discussion of the Alabama claims in the House of Commons and was asked if the state would defray the expenses of Livingstone's funeral. The following week Parliament agreed to release funds to cover the costs of transporting the body from Southampton docks to London and its burial in Westminster Abbey. Livingstone was to be granted a state funeral, with all due pomp and circumstance. Livingstone's death and burial were widely reported in America too. *The Times* reported, 'The secretary of the American Geographical Society has sent a telegram to Mr Clements R. Markham, asking the exact hour and day of the funeral, in order that the event may be celebrated on both sides of the Atlantic simultaneously.'

The town of Southampton threw itself into feverish organisation:

> During the landing of the corpse and its progress from the docks to the railway station, minute guns are to be fired from the platform battery by gunners of the 1st Hants Artillery Volunteers, muffled peels are to be rung by the church bells, flags hoisted half-mast on shore and afloat, and a band will play the 'Dead March' in *Saul* … A mortuary chapel is to be fitted up at the railway station for the temporary reception of the remains.

The Lord Mayor would be there in full regalia, and – of course – Stanley would be present too. A special train was to be 'supplied by the London and South-Western Railway Company' and 'the shops along the route [would be] partially closed'. In fact, it proved rather a tricky enterprise, as all these elaborate arrangements had to be held in suspense awaiting the arrival of the *Malwa*, and the ship did not dock as expected on 13 April, causing some consternation: 'unless the landing of the body was to be divested of all ceremonial, it must be deferred'. It was unthinkable that the ceremonials should be abandoned, so everything was held back. On the wet and windy morning of 15 April the approach of the *Malwa* was signalled from Hurst Castle and at about eight o'clock she arrived in Southampton Water. The telegraph operators started eagerly tapping out the news.

Livingstone's coffin, which had travelled in the mail room of the *Malwa* 'covered with the Penisular and Oriental Company's flag', was taken on board the landing craft, the *Queen*, and a 'wreath of camellias and other flowers was placed on the coffin, now covered with the Union Jack, as it lay on the deck'. Before it was disembarked, the coffin was draped yet again and 'enveloped in the usual velvet pall, fringed with white silk', it was carried to the hearse. Jacob Wainwright walked behind the coffin, but he 'was not the only African who walked behind the hearse. Another negro, bearing a white banner with a black border, and the words "Livingstone, the friend of the Slave," fell into position as the procession reached the Quay.' All the press reports insist on how orderly the crowd was as it watched the procession. These two facts together are intriguing. Where did the African holding the banner come from? Who was he? Certainly, his banner politicised the procession, and, in the wake of the Second Reform Act of 1867, which had given the vote to more people in Britain than ever before, there was

13. Jacob Wainwright on board the Malwa *with Livingstone's coffin.*

a nervousness about the ways in which the people would behave in a newly extended democracy.

A few minutes after three p.m. a special train pulled out of Southampton and took the body and Livingstone's close associates to Waterloo Station in London. There they were met by another hearse and mourning coaches which took everyone on to the RGS headquarters in Savile Row. That evening, the surgeon Sir William Fergusson and others inspected the body in order to identify it as Livingstone's, as 'many were sceptical as to this dead frame being that of Livingstone'. But Fergusson announced, 'The identification was placed beyond doubt, the left arm still showing traces of a fracture caused by the bite of a lion more than thirty years ago.' And – like Egyptian grave goods – 'There were also found the doctor's gold-banded cap and Mr Stanley's card.' William Webb was present and was quite 'unmanned' by the sight of the body, 'as, apart from the broken arm, there was not the slightest doubt as to the identity, both face and features being perfectly recognizable'.

THE FUNERAL

David Livingstone's funeral took place in Westminster Abbey at one p.m. on Saturday 18 April, and was an elaborate affair. His remains had been 'transferred from the rough coffin of Zanzibar wood ... to a coffin of English oak', so that the Scot who had lived most of his life in Africa was now quite literally 'repackaged' as 'English'. His body was not returned to 'his people' – his family in the Lowlands of Scotland – but to a public space in London. Livingstone had become the property of the nation – part of its heritage and its history, part of the 'long bead-roll of England's worthies who now repose in Westminster Abbey'. But which nation? The music played during the service was all conspicuously English – Croft, Purcell and Tallis. It would have been perfectly possible to give Livingstone a public funeral in Glasgow: in December 1853, for example, Livingstone's old theology tutor, Ralph Wardlaw, had been buried at the public expense in the Glasgow Necropolis, one of the new burial grounds being established outside large cities in the nineteenth century. Was Livingstone's internment inside Westminster Abbey intended to make Scotland feel part of the 'centre', or was it just ignoring Scotland with an arrogant English imperialism that swallowed all differences into itself? On top of the coffin was placed 'a wreath of azaleas and other choice flowers' as a 'tribute of respect and admiration from Queen Victoria'. The Queen also sent an empty coach to the funeral, as was customary, and many dignitaries attended in person. At one level, the funeral was staged as a dignified celebration of empire of a kind that the Tory Prime Minister, Disraeli, was keen to promote to the British public in this period. Livingstone was described as 'the great explorer' – and not 'missionary' – and his grave was placed among those of military men. It was dug immediately opposite the monument of Field-Marshal Wade, and next to the grave of Major Rennell, a soldier and founder of the Society for African Exploration. Whatever its misgivings about him in life, in death Livingstone was welcomed into the elite and ruling class of England, and particularly into a politically conservative account of empire.

But there were other ways of reading the funeral too. Significant among the mourners was the anti-slavery campaigner Sir Fowell Buxton, the grandson of Thomas Fowell Buxton, who had inspired Livingstone back in the 1840s. The radical MP John Bright was also present, as were other notable radicals and critics of the empire. Even as the funeral staged the triumphalist power of empire and of 'England', the forces of resistance and criticism were present. This was indeed a highly politicised occasion in which Livingstone was symbolically connected with the campaign against slavery and radical British politics. The Paris correspondent of *The Times* reported, 'The Radicals [in France] have expressed themselves much aggrieved that Michelet was not honoured with such a public funeral as Livingstone, and this question … has given rise to bitter recriminations and comparisons between Westminster Abbey and the Panthéon.' Michelet was a revolutionary French historian, author of *Le Peuple* (1846), who was also born in humble circumstances and furthered himself through his own efforts, and who died in 1874. The fact that the French drew parallels between him and Livingstone tells us that, while Livingstone could be seen as an establishment figure and a servant of empire, he could also be claimed as a radical and a hero of the people, and in this double-jointedness we can discern the makings of his future life as a remarkably pliable and adaptable icon.

The whole spectacle of the funeral drew attention as much to the mourners as to the mourned. In fact, after mid-century, the culture of mourning in both Britain and America did become more public and more focused on the grief of the mourners than on the deceased. The funerals of the rich become more elaborate and choreographed, as sincerity was no longer seen as indivisible from privacy. Livingstone's funeral procession made its way down St James's Street, 'where a deputation of working men obtained permission to add, in the name of their order, a laurel wreath ... to the other decorations on the coffin'. The people in the dense crowd along the route took off their hats 'reverently' as the coffin passed. The 'neighbourhood of the Abbey' was so crowded that the police had work hard to keep a route through the throng open. 'All ranks, from the very highest to the humblest in the land, vied in paying him honour.' If we can believe the newspaper reports, many in the crowd were weeping. William Cotton Oswell's wife recorded in her diary that it was 'such a sight as I shall never forget, the sea of heads and the long train of carriages, filling Broad Sanctuary, representing every grade of life, from the Queen to the humblest crossing-sweeper ... The concentrated, *cumulated* feeling was ... deeply moving.' Why? What was it about Livingstone that unlocked such recognition and such public grief? Was this a religious or a secular reaction to his death? Later, reviewing Waller's edition of Livingstone's *Last Journals*, *The Times* said, 'In the Journals before us there is scarcely a trace of missionary exertion – none of missionary success', and the *Saturday Review* focused on 'the moral grandeur of Livingstone's character' rather than on his religious beliefs. The crowd seemed to be engaged more in hero-worship than in religious meditation, although the two, of course, are not necessarily mutually exclusive. But was Livingstone's celebrity the result of a secularising culture in the 1870s? Was this outpouring of public grief about the need to find new repositories of value as religious faith waned? Or did Livingstone also represent something more specific for those ordinary people who turned out to pay their last respects on that sunny April day? On the occasion of the Duke of Wellington's funeral, Carlyle had commented that Wellington was 'the *last* perfectly honest and brave man', and Tennyson had written an ode in which he declared sadly, 'The last great Englishman is low.' But Livingstone did not represent the last great Englishman: he may have represented some lost opportunities, but his popular hero status probably rested more on the fact that he was *not* representative of any kind of generic 'type' – neither an 'honest brave man' nor a 'great Englishman'. After all, he had always been somewhat at odds with the various institutions he was supposed to represent – the RGS, the Church, the British Empire – and it was perhaps this opposition that endeared him to the people: he had never been quite one of 'them' in the establishment; he had remained singular, an individual.

Oswell wrote, 'He had so nearly done his work, but not quite', and now Livingstone's work would never be completed. Even as he was being laid to rest, Britain was beginning to toughen up its imperial interventions in Africa. Throughout 1873 and 1874 the second Asante Expedition, led by Garnet Joseph Wolseley (who was the inspiration for the 'Modern-Major-General' of Gilbert and Sullivan's 1879 operetta *The Pirates of Penzance*), filled the newspapers. In August 1873 Wolseley was sent to lead an expedition to punish Asante incursions into the Gold Coast protectorate by seizing their capital city, Kumasi. Stanley was sent to cover the story for the *New York Herald*. Wolseley accomplished the goal with great efficiency and economy, conducting a model campaign, and burned Kumasi to the ground. In 1879 the Anglo-Zulu War flared up suddenly. Further British expeditions against the Asante were to take place in 1896 and 1900, the latter leading to the British annexation of the territory. By 1900, too, Britain would be engaged in the Boer War in South Africa.

BLACK FACES IN VICTORIAN BRITAIN

But what of the conspicuous presence of Jacob Wainwright, Kalulu and the anonymous banner-wielding African in Britain in 1874? Right through the nineteenth century, from 1810, when Sara Baartman ('the Hottentot Venus') was shown in London, black Africans were put on display as exhibits in Britain. In 1852 the *Illustrated London News* announced the arrival in England of 'two little savages from the Orange River ... these interesting little natives of the land of Bushmen, Hottentots and Kaffirs have been rescued from the lowest depths of barbarism and [are now] surrounded by the novel sights and sounds, and comforts of English civilisation'. These 'Earthmen' were displayed in London.

Throughout the summer of 1853 the 'Zulu Kaffirs' caused a sensation at St George's Gallery, Knightsbridge, where they performed a highly dramatic show on an elaborate set painted to look like their 'native land' near Natal. In their traditional African dress, they acted out a meal scene, a hunt, a witchdoctor scene, a wedding and so on. They were a huge success and both the 'Earthmen' and the Zulus were commanded to perform before Queen Victoria and her children. The press were astonished at the Zulu troupe, who seemed such 'naturally good actors' and gave 'a performance more natural and less like acting'. As we shall see, the problem of authenticity and imitation was one which could always be guaranteed to accompany any display of black Africans in the nineteenth century.

Britain had experienced other kinds of black performance too. Frederic Douglass, then still a fugitive African slave from the States, made a splash in 1845–7, when he gave more than 300 lectures across Britain attacking American slavery. Douglass was extremely articulate, dressed as a gentleman and was welcomed in liberal abolitionist circles as an acquaintance and a dinner guest. The printed slave narratives, such as Douglass's, had been circulating very widely throughout the century, and – as the *Athenaeum* had remarked in a review of John Brown's 1855 *Slave Life in Georgia* – were popular partly because of their sensational and violent content: 'the stereotyped account of horrors, and nothing less than sickening amplifications on the effect of the bull-whip and the cobbling-ladle'. Certainly, much of the popular interest in slave narratives, which were eagerly consumed in penny parts, and the long queues to view actual fugitive slaves were partly inspired by a curiosity that verged on prurience. Touring African-Americans would sometimes show the scars on their backs from whippings, or exhibit the torture instruments used by slavers to the audience. To many Americans at the time, their celebrity in Britain seemed absurd. The *New York Express* was incredulous about the British enthusiasm for the African-American visitor: 'All his movements are chronicled, all his sayings reported, his profile is done in mezzotint, and circulated, the old ladies invite him to their tea-drinkings, and the young ones exclaim "what a dear!"'

Another runaway slave, Henry 'Box' Brown, came to England in 1851, after escaping from the American South to the North hidden in a small box. He appeared in music halls all over Britain, often re-enacting his escape as publicity for his show: 'He was packed up in the box at Bradford about half-past five o'clock, and forwarded to Leeds by the six o'clock train.' When he then jumped out of the box onstage, the audience were 'wide-mouthed and wonder-gaping'. Much of Henry 'Box' Brown's act was calculated to ridicule the 'democracy' of America. Much more common, though, in mid-Victorian Britain than the African-American shows were the 'blackface' shows. American and British white men, 'blacked up' with burnt cork, would perform 'Nigger Minstrel' shows. The American 'Ethiopian Serenaders', for example, toured their immensely popular show from the late 1840s onwards in Britain, and there were many other imitators. These minstrel shows were attended by the middle classes as well as the working classes and their influence on British stereotypes of race was undoubtedly immense. Indeed, this was not just a Victorian phenomenon: the BBC's *Black and White Minstrel Show* ran from 1958 right up until 1978. Frederic Douglass blamed the 'pestiferous Ethiopian minstrels' for anti-American prejudice in Britain in 1859.

Douglass saw himself as a completely different kind of performer, but in fact, for the majority of the British public, the distinctions were probably not always so clear. These acts – both African-American and 'blackface' – reached extraordinarily diverse audiences in Britain. While Frederic Douglass was a serious campaigner for abolition, Henry 'Box' Brown's act was the sensational stuff of music hall, but both reached a wide popular audience. Indeed, it could be argued that Brown's performance was as political as Douglass's in his use of a painted panorama which showed slaves being sold in front of 'Liberty Hall'. Black servants had been fashionable in Britain in the mid-eighteenth century – Dr Johnson, for example, much esteemed his black servant, Francis Barber, and left him a pension in his will. But it seems that the 'indigenous' black population of Britain had begun to decline during the late eighteenth century, so black faces were becoming a less and less common sight on the streets in the Victorian period, and probably were most often seen around the docklands of Liverpool, Bristol and London. Some of the whites who queued to see Frederic Douglass, while professedly there for spotless evangelical and abolitionist reasons, were undoubtedly also eager to see this curiosity – an articulate black. Similarly, some of the people who went to see Henry 'Box' Brown, while professedly just looking for a good evening out, may have come away shocked at what was happening in their 'brother country', the United States. The point is that the lines between freak show, comedy and political lecture were blurry. Blatant racism was – oddly to our modern way of thinking – not necessarily a block to sympathy with the 'negro' cause in the mid-Victorian period.

In the spring of 1873 the Fisk Jubilee Singers arrived in

Britain from Nashville and made a big impact. They were among the first to perform 'Negro Spirituals' in public – the slave songs of the plantations. Their first concert was on 12 May in the Queen's Concert Rooms, Hanover Square, and they stayed in Britain for a year, leaving in May 1874. Posters, billboards and whole columns of advertisements in *The Times* announced their concerts and they had become a major sensation by the time of Livingstone's funeral. When they sang at a private party given by the Duke of Argyle on a rainy spring day, Queen Victoria arrived on a family visit and was fascinated to find the singers there: 'They sing extremely well together,' she recorded in her journal, and they are 'real negroes' – by which she presumably meant that they were not blackface minstrels. But the Fisk's soprano, Maggie Porter, was less sure as to whether Victoria was a 'real' queen: 'I received the greatest disappointment of my life. The Queen wore no crown, no robes of state. She was like many English ladies I had seen in her widow's cap and weeds.' While they themselves were being inspected and stared at, these African-American visitors were scrutinising Britain with just as much interest.

The immense celebrity of the Fisk Jubilee Singers and the 'blackface' acts touring Britain in the 1870s probably helped to fuel a revival of the ethnological exhibitions and shows at this time. During the Zulu War of 1879, the American stunt-man and entrepreneur Farini (William Leonard Hunt) exhibited 'Farini's Friendly Zulus', which worked beautifully as a ploy to revive flagging public interest in London's Royal Aquarium, which he was managing at the time – crowds turned out in their droves to see these semi-naked men throwing their deadly spears. The variety of black faces in the public sphere in Britain gives an important context to the 'tours' of Livingstone's black servants in the same period. While the abolitionists had used a picture of an enchained black man with the motto 'Am I not a Man and a Brother?' on their publicity material, there was considerable disagreement as to quite what the black brother should become after emancipation. First Jacob and then Susi and Chuma were invited over to Britain to be honoured for their heroic loyalty to Livingstone. When they arrived in England, though, their status became uncomfortably unclear. Were they noble or savage? Were they honoured guests? Or were they servants? Could they speak for themselves or were they better advised to speak only when asked a question? Were they tourists, here on holiday to tour the country and see it, or were they exhibits, here to tour the country and be seen by it? Were they, too, allowed to be explorers and discoverers of a strange and foreign land, or was that role exclusively preserved for white European men?

LIVINGSTONE'S AFRICAN SERVANTS

So, when Livingstone's black servants arrived in Britain, they were both a novelty and not a novelty. Three of them travelled to Britain in 1874 and toured around the country. There is very scanty evidence of what they did, and almost none of what they thought of what the *Illustrated London News* had termed 'the novel sights and sounds, and comforts of English civilisation'. While the British press made the three servants into highly sentimentalised emblems of fidelity, loyalty and obedience, it is likely that they themselves would have explained their long journey to the coast with Livingstone's body somewhat differently. Perhaps they had seen Livingstone as a kind of patron, and a channel to

14. *Livingstone's funeral in Westminster Abbey as depicted in the* Illustrated London News, *with Jacob Wainwright in the forefront of the composition.*

larger resources: they were plainly cosmopolitans too.

The two Africans in the funeral procession – Wainwright and Stanley's African boy, Kalulu – were much noticed in the newspaper coverage in America and Britain. Wainwright had been interviewed by the *New York Herald* at Suez on his way back with Livingstone's body. They both travelled in the second mourning coach with Kirk and Webb, preceding Stanley, who was in the third, with Waller, Oswell and Young. Wainwright was also a coffin-bearer. In the absence of an illustration, his name was followed by '(negro)' in *The Times*, whereas the *Illustrated London News* made him a focal point of its illustration of the funeral. *The Times* described him as 'the figure which appeared to excite most curiosity', and dwelt on the image of Wainwright poring over his prayer book by Livingstone's graveside as the Dean intoned 'Earth to earth, ashes to ashes ...' After the coffin was lowered into the grave, Wainwright threw in a palm branch as a symbol of Africa. *The Times* published a poem by Lord Houghton (Richard Monckton Milnes) called 'Ilala' which – significantly – focused its last verse exclusively on the fidelity of Livingstone's African servants:

> Mornings of sympathy and trust
> For such as bore
> Their master's spirit's sacred crust
> To England's shore.

Livingstone's obituary in *The Times* noticed Livingstone's unusual relationship with Africans: 'Above all, his success depended, from first to last, in an eminent degree upon the great power which he possessed of entering into the feelings, wishes, and desires of the African tribes and engaging their hearty sympathy.' The word 'sympathy' suggests a reciprocity in Livingstone's relationships with Africans which was unheard of at the time. Livingstone did seek backing from the British government to found British colonies in Central and East Africa, but he never got it, and it would be crude and wrong to think of him as a straightforward Victorian colonialist. He lived with African people for much longer than any other explorer. What makes him interesting now is perhaps not so much his heroic reputation as his frailties and mistakes. Livingstone was often unsure where exactly in Africa he was, he was sometimes crawling – literally – along in the mud, sometimes desperately ill, sometimes hallucinating. If we examine his story closely, it rather complicates the simple idea we often have of Victorian empire as being characterised by the paternalistic export of British values into 'other' places. In fact, it was the enormous and generous effort of Africans that kept Livingstone alive by hosting him within their communities. Livingstone increasingly allowed himself to be taken care of in this way, and his growing understanding of his own weakness and frailty in the place counteracts any simple 'empire story'. Indeed, he came to believe that the business of 'civilising' Africa would take much longer than he had originally thought, because he had not counted on there being so much *there* in Africa already. By 1862 Livingstone's historical scale for the Africa project has extended dramatically: 'Some may be disposed to sneer at the idea of Negroes ever becoming as civilised as ourselves,' he says, 'forgetting apparently that no great time has elapsed since our forefathers were famous for burning witches or that it was missionary agency that put a stop to English youths being sold as slaves at Rome.'

Speaking in Glasgow in 1874, a few days before Livingstone's death was announced, Sir Bartle Frere, the President of the Royal Geographical Society, had referred to 'questionings as to the degree in which I suppose he has naturalised himself and become like one of the Africans'. Livingstone never 'naturalised' himself or 'went native' in the ways so grotesquely and obsessively imagined and feared by the British administrators of empire. His journals show almost the opposite dynamic, revealing an increasing awareness of his status as a guest in Africa, and an increasing gratitude and admiration for the people who chose to care for him there. The truth is that it was never entirely clear what exactly Livingstone *was* doing in Africa. His original employers, the London Missionary Society, gave up on him as a missionary, the RGS never fully accepted him as an explorer, and it seems that his British governmental position as a 'Roving Consul', while it involved lots of roving, and some writing of reports when he felt there was something to report, had no other onerous duties attached.

In 1889 Waller reported, 'We are told that no tomb is visited so often as that of Livingstone in Westminster Abbey. Men of all nations stand and spell out the words.' In 1913, on the hundredth anniversary of Livingstone's birth, a celebratory pamphlet printed a photograph of two black men kneeling at his grave. Inside the pamphlet the writer recalls, 'Sauntering down the aisle of Westminster Abbey ... I saw a sight which impressed me even more than all the sights of London. I came across two negroes, reverently praying, and bowing low on their knees, at the grave of David Livingstone. It was a beautiful and pathetic scene.' On the eve of the First World War, black men are still figured as one of the 'sights' of London, a 'beautiful and pathetic scene', so how were Livingstone's black servants treated when *they* arrived in England in 1874?

Three Africans who had worked for Livingstone visited Britain in 1874. Jacob Wainwright came first for the funeral, and then Susi and Chuma travelled over together. Wainwright was brought over by the LMS and used as a promotional speaker for the missionary cause – it is not clear whether he was paid or not. Susi and Chuma were brought over by Horace Waller and James 'Paraffin' Young, and were contracted and paid to help with the editing of Livingstone's *Last Journals*.

What emerges from this account is the enormous amount of information that is lost for ever. The only record we have of what these Africans did in Britain is left in traces in the letters and journals of their British hosts. The main source for this chapter is William Webb's daughter Augusta's memoirs of the men's visits to Newstead Abbey. As an adult, Augusta Fraser accompanied her husband to Jamaica in 1892, and under the pseudonym 'Alice Spinner' she published novels and stories, and later wrote a memoir of Livingstone. As with all memoirs, it is difficult to know how much of her account is exact, but there is a delightful sense of being shown behind the scenes in *Livingstone and Newstead* (1913). Anyway, we have absolutely no record of what the servants really thought or felt, possibly because nobody asked them; and certainly, even if they did, nobody thought their answers were worth recording.

The closest we can get to the Africans' voices is by looking at Waller's marbled dictation notebook, in which he wrote down the witness accounts of Susi and Chuma as research for his *Last Journals*. His writing is hasty and scrawled, not like the neat hand of his letters, as he hurried to keep up with their stories, and some of the rhythm of their speech survives in his notes. They mostly spoke to him in English, although he could speak several African languages. There are moments when the texture of their experience shines through vividly, as when Susi tells him that, nursing Livingstone in the night, he 'had to hold candle close to the label till he got right medicine'. Two letters survive that were written from England by Jacob Wainwright, although it seems that they have been corrected by the Rev. W. Price and were probably written under his scrutiny. But these are tiny shreds of evidence and in the end this is a chapter about a silence. Nevertheless, some attention to the gap where the servants' stories might have been may perhaps help to remind us just how difficult it was for British observers in 1874 to grasp the complexities of African identity.

JACOB WAINWRIGHT

In reality, Jacob Wainwright was far from a blank. Young though he was, he had already had a turbulent life which had created a complex identity for him. It was also as 'modern' a life as that of any of the Europeans in this story, and blows to pieces the Victorian – but surprisingly persistent – notion that Africans somehow lived in an earlier, simpler time. This young man negotiated dislocation not just from his birthplace but from all his tribal connections and culture. He travelled and lived in three different continents, thus experiencing his own relationship to growing capitalist world markets in a shockingly direct way; he witnessed technological innovations, such as steamboats, steam trains, photography, the gaslighting and central heating that Webb had had installed at Newstead Abbey; and he was exposed to startlingly different conceptions of selfhood and individuality in Britain from those he had been used to in Africa and even in India. He was born a Yao in Nyasaland (now Malawi) and a Muslim, as the Sultanate of Zanzibar dominated the east coast and Islam had reached East Africa generations before European influence and Christianity. In the nineteenth century, as one Africanist puts it, 'It emerged that Yao identity was rather slippery. Indeed, the more one probed back into Yao oral history the less substantial the Yao appeared.' As a child, Jacob Wainwright had been bought as a slave, probably sold by his own people, who responded to an increased demand for labour in the sugar trade by supplying slaves and selling them on the coast near Kilwa. But Wainwright was liberated by the British Coastal Squadron, which patrolled and intercepted slave ships. He was then sent to India to be taught English and Christianity at the Church Missionary Society (CMS) Nasik Asylum, about 100 miles north-east of Bombay.

The Rev. W. Salter Price had founded the Christian village of Sharanpur (city of refuge) in 1854. He also set up the Nasik school and workshops for boys which educated some 200 liberated slaves. In 1860 the Rev. C. W. Isenberg had taken charge of the school and, because he had previously been a missionary in Ethiopia, he took an interest in released and freed slaves and started the policy of taking in Africans as well as Indians. The Nasik school offers another example of the close association of British missionary work in Africa and India at this time. For the young 'Jacob', whose African name is not recorded, the move to India must have been a culture shock of a kind he was to experience again when he was sent to England in 1874. In addition to his African customs and practices, he was a monotheist Muslim, now being taught about Christian theology. His life was a cosmopolitan one as he travelled between cultures and religions.

Early in 1872, in order to get back to Africa, Wainwright responded to a call for servants to join the RGS Livingstone Search & Relief Expedition. He arrived in Zanzibar with five other Nasik youths, including Carus Farrar and Matthew Wellington, to report to Lieutenant Dawson. When that relief party broke up, he and his Nasik colleagues joined the party of fifty-seven men hired by Stanley for Livingstone, and so he travelled with Livingstone, and then with Livingstone's corpse, for a little under two years. The life was tough and hardly a homecoming. Rev. Price happened to be in England when news of Livingstone's death broke. He recognised Jacob Wainwright's name in the reports and telegraphed that he should be sent home with the body. As Augusta Fraser recalls it, 'The idea in the abstract touched the popular feeling, and was eminently right and proper', although she agrees with Horace Waller that Susi and Chuma, who had been with Livingstone for much longer, would have been more appropriate in this role.

The sight of Jacob Wainwright did indeed, as we have seen, 'touch the popular feeling,' and this was exactly why the CMS paid his fare. Wainwright attracted a great deal of press and public interest in late April and early May. 'The youth evinced remarkable quickness and intelligence, and his devotion to Livingstone appears to have been almost romantic ... his shining, dusky, fat face was lit up with a pleasant smile,' reported the *Illustrated London News* upon Wainwright's arrival in Britain. A certain Mr Cowton even named his racehorse 'Jacob Wainwright' that summer. After the funeral, Wainwright travelled around the country in the company of Price, speaking to well-attended meetings about Livingstone and his own experiences of slavery, and helping to fund-raise for the CMS. On 27 April 1874 he attended a large RGS meeting in the theatre of London University, along with Livingstone's son Tom. In May Wainwright attended a CMS anniversary meeting, where Price spoke for him and told his story. Later on his 'tour' he began to speak for himself; at the Queen Street Hall, Edinburgh, in October, for example, Wainwright 'narrated his own history and gave an account of the last days of Livingstone'. Alice Fraser remarked that 'one might not exactly admire the feeling that prompted full material advantage being taken of the public sentiment, and the consequent subscriptions that resulted.' In fact, as we have seen, there was already a long tradition of exhibiting black Africans to the English public, both for publicity for the abolitionist cause and for profit.

An uneasiness about the status of the black servants reveals itself in Augusta Fraser's account of Wainwright's visit to Newstead Abbey in June 1874. When slated to appear at a large meeting in Nottingham, he was brought to Newstead by Price to meet Webb and his family and guests. They arrived just before lunchtime on a hot June day, and Augusta Fraser recalls, 'It was the demeanour of Jacob that most amazed my father, and was a distinct shock to us all.' They had already seen him at the funeral, so, she says, already knew that he was 'remarkably ugly, being almost an exaggerated Negro type', unlike two other of Livingstone's African servants, Susi and Chuma, who had just left Newstead. But they were horrified that, 'during the two months that had elapsed since the funeral, he had deteriorated markedly in manners and behaviour ... He thrust himself forward in conversation in an unlooked-for way, and unless he was the center of attention, was undisguisedly annoyed and sulky.' Fraser, like Livingstone, felt that 'Negro servants' should be kept 'under kindly but due discipline', and an extremely awkward lunch followed, as it dawned on the family that Wainwright was expecting to sit with them at table: 'To be fair to him I must say he had learnt good "table manners", as they say in America, and managed his knife and fork with skill.'

Later that afternoon, Fraser reports:

> Tom [Livingstone] had been sitting in the billiard room in the afternoon when Jacob had come in asking for brandy. He had refused to give him any, or there wouldn't have been a missionary meeting that evening at all ... growing unpleasantly and gratuitously confidential, he imparted into Tom's disgusted ears the great boredom of his present life, which he could only endure because at that time there seemed no way out of it. He added the hope of better things in the future, as once back in Africa he

expected to be his own master, and to have, among other advantages, the means of procuring a great many wives!

As the family had been told earlier by Price that Wainwright was likely to be a missionary, this aspiration dismayed them. They would have been further dismayed had they known that he was still a practising Muslim.

Perhaps the story would sound a little different if we could hear it from Wainwright's lips. Already having suffered the trauma of slavery, wrenched from his family, he had been sent to India and then had spent two brutalising years on tough expeditions. And now he found himself trailing around another strange new country with the sanctimonious Price. Buttoned up on a hot June day in 'a dark semi-clerical costume', eating strange food with alien instruments, and forced constantly to perform to people he had never met before and would never meet again, both in social settings and at crowded meetings, who treated him as a spectacle and an exhibition, it seems perfectly reasonable that he might not have been having the time of his life. In a stilted letter written from London in May, he says, 'I have to remain in England for a few months more', which hardly makes him sound like an enthusiastic tourist. Fraser herself acknowledges that it was Price's idea, and clearly not Wainwright's, that he should be ordained a missionary and work in East Africa. But Wainwright, as 'the low class' African that Webb pronounced him, could have no higher aspiration than to escape this new form of servitude, to become 'his own master'. Tom Livingstone, who – we are told – held 'a light post in some business house in Egypt' and was on leave at the time, did not perhaps spend much time reflecting on the relative trials of Wainwright's existence and his own.

In fact, Fraser's reactions to Wainwright are revealing. While she allows that he exhibits signs of westernised culture, she immediately denigrates this as facile 'copying'. He had learned his table manners, like his conversation, as 'a mere parrot echo' of those around him, displaying 'the extraordinary facility for imitation of his race'. His 'set speech on, of course, the most conventional lines' at the Nottingham meeting is enthusiastically reported in the morning paper the next day, and she adds, 'I believe he was, to do him justice, wonderfully fluent, having the excellent word-memory of most negroes.' But if Africans who behaved too much like Englishmen were mere comic imitators, how were the missionaries ever to know when a 'conversion' to Christianity and western values was genuine? While Wainwright in his inappropriate and 'unbecoming' clerical dress may have seemed comic to the British, how were they to know that the joke was not ultimately on them? The uneasiness around Wainwright is a muddled one – he is both black and a servant. Some of the family's uneasiness seems to relate less to his colour (this was, after all, an exceptional family, close friends of Livingstone's, concurring in his view of 'the stupid prejudice against colour') and more to his class, and to the wider anxieties about servants in the period. Susi and Chuma, for example, had visited Newstead a few weeks previously, and had been far more welcome because they 'knew their place':

> directly they had recovered from their slight embarrassment, they answered all questions put to them, not only in fair English, but with a modest readiness that pleased everyone, upstairs and downstairs alike. From our maids, also, we learnt that their good manners at meal times,

and their quickness at conforming to English habits had impressed the English servants immensely.

Susi and Chuma spoke only when spoken to, ate with the servants downstairs and 'conform[ed] to English habits' rather than 'parroting' their hosts. In fact, Victorian middle-class anxieties about servants getting above themselves were much the same as their anxieties about black people getting above themselves: a similarity which is reflected in the popular humour of the period. What were called 'coon' jokes in the nineteenth century often pivoted on the idea of the black dandy taking on 'airs and graces', and servant jokes used the same trope. Fraser summed up Wainwright's imposture: 'Now we have it on the authority of Proverbs, that among the four things that the earth cannot bear is "a servant when he reigneth," and Jacob Wainwright was of this truth a complete example, for he had evidently grown so much above himself, and was so conceited, that his new manner was painful to witness.' But poor Jacob was also taken to Windsor Castle to visit the Queen, who 'presented me a beautiful book' – possibly a Bible. Can he really be blamed for his confusion as to his proper 'place' in British society?

Wainwright returned to Africa after five months. He clearly longed to get back. His stay in England seems to have distressed him, perhaps because of the confusing contradictions between his celebrity and his servant status. It appears that he travelled back to Mombasa with Price. In January 1876 Price reported from Frere Town, Kenya, that 'Jacob is a great help in teaching' African Christians, but he seems to have drifted away from the mission after a while. Maybe this was what Fraser refered to as his 'missionary career', which she called 'a total failure'. When Stanley returned to East Africa in 1874, he judged Wainwright unsuitable to join his expedition. It is not clear why – possibly Jacob was drinking too much, as Susi certainly was. The life of the servant on African explorations was pretty much like the life of a mercenary soldier and had similarly brutalising effects. The traveller Joseph Thomson reported from Zanzibar in 1879 that 'Jacob Wainwright we found to have fallen considerably. When I last heard of him he was acting as door-porter to one of the Zanzibar traders.' But it seems that in 1880 Wainwright's luck changed and he was recruited by the Rev. Philip O'Flaherty, a CMS missionary on his way to Uganda, who was pleased 'to save this young man from the evil surroundings of Zanzibar' (which Livingstone always called 'Stinkibar'). Wainwright and O'Flaherty reached Rubaga on 18 March 1881. O'Flaherty wrote in his journal about 'Jacob Wainwright, who is a great comfort to me', and he added, 'J.W. is my schoolmaster, interpreter, personal servant and friend.' Unlike Fraser, then, O'Flaherty was not troubled by collapsing the boundary between 'servant' and 'friend'. It seems that Wainwright's view of the relationship may have been somewhat different, though, as on Christmas Day 1881 O'Flaherty rather sadly wrote, 'Jacob Wainwright of Livingstone fame lately my schoolmaster and personal attendant ... was bribed to leave me I learn now by the Arabs.' Jacob's status as servant (and not slave) meant that he was able to leave O'Flaherty's service for higher pay in Mutesa's, and he did – perhaps the categories of service and friendship are not as easily confused by the servant as they are by the master. Mutesa was not 'Arab' in fact, but the ruler of Buganda, a black African who had converted to Islam. In 1891 there was a further sighting of Wainwright at a LMS mission at Urambo in Tanzania, where he died in April 1892.

LIVINGSTONE'S SERVANT PROBLEMS: SUSI, CHUMA AND WEKOTANI

Wainwright was not in Livingstone's service for long, but what of Susi and Chuma, who had been with him every single day since 1866? The story of their visit to Britain is altogether different, although some of the same anxieties attended their appearance. In 1861 Chuma and another boy, Wekotani, had been rescued by Livingstone, who apparently sawed off their slave chains with his own hands. They were both about eleven years old at the time. Wekotani was the son of a chief. Chuma was another Yao like Wainwright, the son of Chimilengo, a skilled fisherman, and Chinjeriapi, who had lived in Kusogwe. He had been sold for two bundles of fish as a slave. On 10 December 1865 the two boys were baptised by Dr Wilson in the presence of Livingstone as John Wekotani and James Chuma, although Carus Farrar reported in 1874 that 'Chuma and Suse in spite of all that the Dr did for them in getting them English education at Dr Wilson's school at Bombay have at last turned out Mohammedans also', a sentence which probably explains why his narrative was not published or widely distributed in Britain at the time. Abdullah Susi was older than the other two – he was already a Zambezi riverman when he joined Livingstone at Shupanga in 1863 to help put together the pieces of the *Lady Nyasa* and to sail her to Bombay the following year. When the ill-fated Zambezi Expedition was recalled in 1863, Livingstone left most of his African servants in Bombay; Wekotani and Chuma were entrusted to Dr Wilson's care at his Free Church College.

When Livingstone returned to Bombay on 11 September 1865, he found only a few of the Africans still alive. Chuma and Wekotani, who had been boarded with a Christian family, had made good progress in Dr Wilson's school, but of the Shupanga men, just Chiko, Amoda and Susi had survived. Livingstone set sail for Africa from Bombay on 5 January 1866. He took no Europeans with him, but he had engaged some sepoys in Poona. He recorded in his diary, 'I mean to … make this a Christian expedition, telling a little about Christ wherever we go.' On the journey, he employed local men, who were good workers but would only engage themselves for a few days at a time – Livingstone's notebook is full of names of the 200 and more men he temporarily employed between April and early June 1866. The sepoys were a disaster, but possibly because of a misunderstanding – they were military men and had expected to be defending the expedition, not carrying the loads themselves. And the loads were considerable: seventy pounds was the customary maximum weight for a porter, who also carried his own baggage. In addition, heavy brass wire used for barter was carried in coils at each end of a pole between two men. Sometimes the men would be required to carry heavy wooden canoes or bits of a disassembled steamboat. Each day began at four a.m., with a stop at five a.m. for breakfast. Halt would be taken at about eight a.m. and the march would be ended by midday, when the heat became intolerable. Dinner was eaten at about four p.m. and everyone turned in about eight p.m., although apparently the women sometimes stayed up later talking.

Livingstone had finally to dismiss the mutinous sepoys, but he had trouble with his home-grown servants too. 'Chuma and Wikatani are very good boys but still boys utterly,' he wrote to Waller in November 1866. He tried to make them his personal servants, but this proved tricky: 'I had them about me personally till I was reduced to last fork and spoon ... They showed an inveterate tendency to lose my things & preserve their own. If I did not shout for breakfast I got it sometime between eleven and two o'clock. I had to relieve them of all charge of my domestic affairs.' In truth the boys were now sixteen and behaving just as sixteen-year-old boys probably always have. Livingstone writes with all the impotence of the master: 'Wikatani was at that stage when civilized boys assume tailed coats. He *would* wear a night shirt I gave him Arab fashion, and if not engaged in an everlasting giggle or smoking in which he screamed in a most disagreeable fashion, was sure to be singing Dididey dididey or Weeweewee.' What the boys were smoking was marijuana ('bange') – and on several occasions they had to be hauled away from such absorbing recreational activities. On 13 April 1867, for example, Livingstone had trouble mobilising the men, who were enjoying the hash and the prostitutes too much to want to move on. Livingstone sighs over the boys' 'excessive levity' and recounts one occasion when 'thieves ... kept up a succession of jokes with Chuma and Wikatani and when the latter was enjoying them, gaping to the sky, they were busy putting the things of which he had charge under their clothes'. It is striking, when reading Livingstone's accounts of camp life, how much African laughter rings through the pages. While Livingstone moans about his servant problems, his servants are laughing.

When Wekotani decided to marry and leave his service, Livingstone was regretful and wrote to Horace Waller: 'I gave him some cloth – a flint gun instead of a percussion one, paper to write to you and, commending him to the chief, bade the poor boy farewell. I was sorry to part with him.' But part with him he must, for a very specific reason: 'Arabs tell the Waiyau chiefs that our objects in liberating slaves is to make them our own and to turn them to our religion. I had declared to them through Wikatani as interpreter that they never become our slaves & were at liberty to go back to their relations if they liked.' It was paramount to Livingstone that the boys remained servants and never behaved as slaves to him. 'A blessing go with him,' he says.

But he was not always so measured in his responses to the servants. He flogged and docked pay from the Nasik boys when they misbehaved, as they often did. In November 1867 Susi, Chuma and several other men ran away, stealing some of the expedition's supplies. Livingstone was furious:

> I resolved to reinstate two. I reject the thief Suzi for he is quite inveterate, and Chuma who ran away 'to be with Suzi' and I who rescued him from slavery, and had been at the expense of feeding and clothing him for years was nobody in his eyes. 'Bange' and black women overcame him, and I feel no inclination to be at further expense and trouble for him.

Livingstone reveals here just how much personal loyalty he expected from his 'freed slaves'. He did soften, and a week or so later he wrote, 'I have taken all the runaways back again – after trying the independent life they will behave better. Much of their ill conduct may be ascribed to seeing that … I was entirely dependent on them – More enlightened people often take advantage of men in similar circumstances … Have faults myself.' Chuma later has to be reprimanded again for looting in the wake of an Arab attack on a native village. In

Stanley's opinion, Susi 'would have been worth his weight in silver if he were not an incorrigible thief'. Livingstone once remarked, on the subject of his servant problems, that his black servants 'acted like the Irish helps in America. The want of a chain to confine them emboldens them.' Again, the status of the emancipated black brother presents problems for the white emancipator. The servants were getting out of hand.

But his servants succoured Livingstone tenderly in his last illness and took no advantage of his frailty. He records many acts of kindness and consideration in his last months of life. On 15 August 1872, for example, he was 'scarcely able to crawl' and he remembered that he 'sat under a tree and Susi came back with coffee and a bit of fowl which revived me'. The men stood by him, too, even when it became clear in Ujiji that there was nothing left to steal – as all Livingstone's stores had been appropriated by the duplicitous Sherif. And it was Susi and Chuma who were largely responsible for carrying Livingstone's body back to the coast, to return him to his people, where they felt he belonged, although he himself had expressed a desire to be buried in Africa, like his wife. Such loyalty is puzzling and does perhaps suggest some real affection for their white-skinned guest, as well as a desire to connect themselves to the wider world.

At the end of May 1874 Susi and Chuma – 'the chiefest mourners' of Livingstone – arrived at Victoria Docks in London. On Friday 29 May 1874 Horace Waller announced to the annual meeting of National Temperance League – in the presence of Tom Livingstone and Henry Stanley – that Susi and Chuma had arrived that day, and that he would have brought them along to the meeting, 'but they were not presentable for want of clothes'. They certainly had clothes, but not western ones. They probably wore Arab clothes on the way over, in fact, but this would have been difficult to explain to a British public, who imagined Africans wearing nothing but a few tufts of feathers. In fact, it probably would have been easier for everyone if they *had* been wearing a few tufts of feathers. The next day, some 'decent' clothes presumably having been hastily procured for them, Susi and Chuma did appear at a meeting of the RGS. Bartle Frere introduced them warmly, congratulating them on their 'duties strenuously performed'. Susi and Chuma then visited the Webbs at Newstead Abbey, where Waller was also staying.

The clothes that were procured for them are interesting. Like Wainwright, Susi and Chuma were dressed in European attire: they both wore 'very thick blue serge jackets, with bright round buttons – reefer jackets, I believe they are called – and blue serge trousers'. But unlike Wainwright, whose 'semi-clerical' outfit was a kind of stage costume, they wore clothes vaguely reminiscent of naval uniforms – utilitarian clothes which sent the signal that they were not on display but rather were there to work. Young, Webb and Waller certainly seem to have agreed in their efforts to avoid displaying the men as African curiosities. Yet an intriguing set of photographs survives, all of which appear to have been taken in the same session by the London society photographers, Maull & Co. Two small albumen carte-de-visite prints picture each of the men in profile, seated at a table in their western suits, both holding walking canes, in a conventional Victorian portrait pose. Chuma even has an English felt hat by his side. But two larger albumen cabinet prints, presumably taken at the same time, picture Chuma and then Chuma and Susi together in African dress, against a painted 'African' backdrop. Chuma has exchanged the felt hat for a feather

15. The portraits of Chuma (top left and right) and Susi (bottom right) that were taken in the same session at Maull & Co. in London in 1874.

headdress and is holding a bow rather than a walking cane. His chest and legs are naked and he is standing, not seated. The photographs taken together summon up an extraordinary scene of Susi and Chuma retiring – perhaps behind a curtain, or to an inner room – to rip off one 'costume' and put on the other. Nothing could have been a more blankly obvious reminder of their uneasy suspension between two cultures but did it worry them? Perhaps not – perhaps they thought it was funny (they laughed a lot, we are told), or perhaps it was all just in a day's work. It is impossible to imagine how Susi and Chuma felt about this quick-change act, but it is worth noting that as far as the studio of Maull & Co. was concerned, there was nothing particularly odd in the bifocality of the images: the photographic cartes-de-visite, which were fashionable as personal calling cards in this period, performed a private function; the cabinet prints, designed to be publicly displayed, performed another.

Another set of photographs was taken of Susi and Chuma in the grounds of Newstead Abbey in a group with Agnes and Tom Livingstone, and Horace Waller. These are oddly informal and rather charming pictures: the group is posed with Livingstone's maps and field maps unfolded around them and, while Susi and Chuma are both standing, in one picture Chuma has his hands on a map on the table in a way which suggests his participation in the imagined conversation. In the other print, Susi and Chuma stand casually at ease, with their hands in their pockets – not at all the proper pose of a servant. Waller is sitting cross-legged upon the ground in both pictures. Altogether these images offer a marked contrast to the very different composition of the carte-de-visite images Stanley had had taken of himself with Kalulu by the London Stereoscopic Company in 1872. In these, Kalulu – a

16. Photograph taken in the grounds of Newstead Abbey in June 1874. From left to right, Agnes Livingstone, Tom Livingstone, Abdullah Susi, James Chuma and Horace Waller.

boy somewhere between nine and eleven years old – is pictured in African dress, head bowed and handing something which could be a card or a cup of coffee to the seated Stanley, who looks sternly back at him from under the brim of his pith helmet. A threatening stick or riding crop is propped against Stanley's knee. It is instantly clear who is in charge, and there is obviously no conversation going on here. Indeed, Stanley used photographs as self-publicity more and more as his fame widened. In 1890 he wrote to an admiring acquaintance, 'I am sorry that I have no photographs with me. To gratify every applicant I should require several

17. Studio portrait of Stanley with Kalulu taken in London around 1872. The caption reads 'Mr. Stanley, in the dress he wore when he met Livingstone in Africa'.

dozen Saratoga trunks.' Stanley had a showman's instinct for instant impact and no scruples about using black Africans to achieve this. When he took Kalulu back to New York in 1872, the poor boy appeared at a press conference dressed up as an 'olde worlde' English pageboy, but at other times he was required to dance 'tribal' dances in African dress, and sing in Swahili to American journalists. No wonder that Kalulu tried to run away from Stanley in 1876; but he was caught, brought back and punished severely.

John Murray, the publisher of Livingstone's *Last Journals*, recorded, 'Chuma & Susi are to be paid at the rate of £5 per month in lieu of wages during their stay in England.' So, on the one hand these were guests and on the other they were also waged workers who were in Britain, importantly, by their own consent. And Susi and Chuma worked hard. June 1874 was hot and sultry, so Waller and Tom Livingstone would conduct their morning interviews with Susi and Chuma out of doors on the grass, instead of in the billiard room, as had originally been planned. Tom wrote that they were 'of immense service to us', for 'they are particularly intelligent, speaking English well. Susi's geographical knowledge is something wonderful and will be of great use in discussing the Tanganyika question [that is, whether Lake Tanganyika fed the Nile or not].' Waller agreed that they were 'actual geographers of no mean attainments'. But they were still treated as servants, whatever their accomplishments. Fraser approved of Waller's manner with them, which was 'considerate, and gentle, but never familiar. They looked up to and respected him in consequence as he deserved.' During their stay they were asked to explain the functions of the various African objects belonging to Livingstone that been sent back to Britain – a task which 'took a considerable amount of time, as everything had to be looked over and compared with the written list made by Jacob Wainwright under Susi's directions at Ilala'. Like the evidence of the group photographs, Waller's serious engagement here with African culture does seem very different from the display of exotica that usually accompanied any tour of native Africans in Britain. Indeed, most nineteenth-century European accounts of travels to Africa show little interest in the material culture of African communities, whereas almost all record the careful inspection of European objects – spectacles, watches, mirrors, shaving equipment – by the Africans. Young, for example, remembers a chief picking his way through his belongings: 'Not the least thing escaped him. I will leave him examining each article of bewonderment.' On the whole, the Europeans did not bother to examine African objects as closely.

Altogether, Susi and Chuma made a much better impression with the Webbs than poor Jacob Wainwright was to do, and Fraser recalls, 'the pleasing and intelligent countenances of Susi and Chumah'. She was particularly captivated by the 'quickness of perception' of Chuma, the younger of the two: 'He was a far more vivacious character, as was easily to be discovered by his bright, dancing, and roving eyes. He appeared to be taking in his novel surroundings with great interest.' Tom Livingstone warmed to the pair and walking around the estate with them, 'he would encourage them to ask questions of all they saw, and give them information about English trees and plants. He used to be greatly diverted by some of their confidences as to the strangeness of English life and ways.' In Fraser's account we are allowed just the tiniest glimpse of Chuma's point of view. 'There was no trifle, however minute, that escaped Chumah's sharp eyes. For example, his bewilderment at having noticed, as he called it, "flour on the face of one of the old English ladies," which to him simply appeared a woeful waste of good food. He was far too unsophisticated to imagine it could be regarded as a beautifier.' It is difficult to peel back the prejudices in which the reported experiences of Chuma are embedded. Chuma was not 'unsophisticated', but just different, and it is possible that he did not exactly think the flour was 'a woeful waste of good food' so much as express – perhaps – his bewilderment at the absurdity of bodily adornment in England, in much the same way as European travellers marvelled at the absurdity of bodily adornment in Africa. This is guesswork, but at the very least we can infer from Fraser's account that

Chuma was not just being looked at but also looking, noticing, comparing and wondering.

Waller took the pair on some edifying outings in London when they came to stay at his vicarage at St John's, Leytonstone – the church in which Livingstone had taken communion before he headed back to Africa for the last time. He took them, for example, to visit the warehouse of a bead dealer in London in order to help him reconstruct the many kinds and colours of beads that Livingstone had carried for barter with Africans. In 1860 Livingstone had written to the UCMA with some helpful suggestions for the missionaries coming out to Africa: 'In beads the fine blue, red, pink, and white are most fashionable among the Manganya – they should all be opaque – clear glass beads must be avoided.' He added a drawing to show a 'good size' of bead – which seemed to be very small, just two or three millimetres in diameter. All we can do is speculate as to what Susi and Chuma made of the bead warehouse. Did seeing that the glass beads, valuable currency in Africa, were so little valued and so very cheap in Britain make them think about what Europeans were up to in Africa? Indeed, economists have a word for this disparity between the value of the material used to mint the currency and the face value of that currency: seigneurage. The seigneurage on glass beads was immense and exploitative.

Waller also took them to an agricultural show, where they compared the Cochin-China fowls and the short-horned cattle to breeds they had observed in Africa on their travels with Livingstone. Another trip was to a workhouse, where Susi and Chuma told the children about slavery in Africa. In his notebook, Waller wrote, '19 June took lads to B Workh saw childs wards – boys & girls in bed – they stood and described how the slave child. were tethered right & left in the big huts.' Again, it is tempting to wonder what Susi and Chuma thought of the modern British way of managing the poor. Jacob Wainwright reports that he was taken to see 'many wonderful works' in Sheffield too, but he does not record his reactions more fully. Livingstone had written, 'To Africans our cotton mills are fairy dreams', but it is tantalising to speculate over what these men made of the conspicuous poverty and misery among what were termed 'the industrial classes' in Britain at this time. In 1848 George Catlin, who toured with a community of North American 'Indians' around Britain, had written, 'I have long since been opposed to parties of Indians being brought to this country, believing that civilization should be a gradual thing, rather than open the eyes of these ignorant people to its mysteries at a glance, when the mass of poverty and vice alarms them.' One wonders how 'civilised' things looked to Livingstone's servants. On 25 June Waller records that Susi and Chuma expressed their desire to return to Africa. Like Wainwright, they seem to have been eager to leave 'civilisation' behind as soon as possible.

In July Susi and Chuma made their 'long-planned visit' to James 'Paraffin' Young at his Kelly Estate in Wemyss Bay, near Glasgow. Presumably they travelled by train. Young was later to construct a miniature version of the Victoria Falls on his estate as a tribute to his dead friend. Fraser reports that when Susi and Chuma arrived, 'It was nearly haytime, and the grass was long and thick in the fields, ... [and] closely resembled the African native grass', and either the men were asked to or they decided to build 'practically the exact copy' of the hut they built for Livingstone at Ilala. They also modelled a copy of the *kilanda* on which they carried Livingstone around when his illness had become acute, and they built

18. *A replica of the hut in which Livingstone died, built by Susi and Chuma on their visit to Britain.*

a small replica of Chitambo's village. A photograph of the hut was sent to Webb, and Waller reproduced it in the *Last Journals*. In September the men visited the Livingstone family at Hamilton and constructed another replica hut. Anna Mary, the younger daughter, wrote to her friend the Danish author Hans Christian Andersen, 'Papa's two coloured servants were here seeing us last week. They were telling us a great many interesting things about Papa, and one of them called Chumah made a little model of the grass hut in which Papa died and showed us the position of Papa's bed in it. It is very interesting to us.' Were they doing this as a performance? Or were they doing it out of a desire to communicate something of Livingstone to his friends and family, and to offer some comfort to them in their grief? Of course it is impossible to tell, just as it would be impossible to tell why most servants in the nineteenth century did the things that they did. No written records survive – just the photograph of the finished hut in which Susi and Chuma do not appear.

While Susi and Chuma were staying with Waller at Leytonstone, they became members of the church choir, despite being Muslims, and attended the national school in the old chapel. As in most middle-class Victorian drawing rooms, in the drawing room of the Leytonstone vicarage was a piano. One day Waller scribbled in his notebook, 'When Chuma had been telling us about the man dying [in captivity, a slave] thinking about his home, Alice [Waller's wife] offered to play for them & played "Home sweet home" and in their astonishment – they had never seen a piano before – they asked if the keys were Ivory! What a flood of thought came up how this Ivory had been subject to the same agony of human heartbreak.' Even through such a mediated account, we can glimpse the shock of these two African men encountering the material culture of Britain: cheap glass beads and piano keys which resonated for them in ways which were completely disjunctive with the culture around them. What did they *do* with the impossible juxtaposition of those heartbroken slaves and the polite tinkling of the ivories in Victorian drawing rooms? We have no idea. The collision of Africa with Britain was not so much the collision of the ancient with the modern, or the savage with the civilised, as it was so often represented at the time, as the collision of modernity with modernity. The African modernity and the British one showed themselves to be fatally linked and utterly incompatible in ways which would only become more brutal as the century wore on. East Africa particularly was in a state of alarming political flux in the late nineteenth century: as Susi reported to Waller, in his part of Africa, the 'people saw only thing to get guns'.

'FAITHFUL TO THE END'

Susi and Chuma were in London with Waller to receive bronze medals at the anniversary meeting of the RGS on 22 June 1874. Sir Bartle Frere gave a sentimental eulogy to Livingstone's 'faithful band' of 'negro followers' whose 'devotion ... whilst it has excited the admiration of every civilized nation, has perhaps done more than any individual act on record to raise the black races in the estimation of the world'. One wonders whether their trip to Britain raised the white races in the estimation of Susi and Chuma, but nobody seems to have worried too much about this. Fraser described Susi and Chuma as 'two big children' and their loyalty and fidelity were figured as like those of children, or dogs. Indeed, she remembers another black servant of her father's, a 'wild Kaffir boy' whom he had nicknamed Smike, who visited the family in England many years after Webb had returned from Africa, and, upon seeing his old master again, started 'to dance and frisk round him more like a great dog, than a grown man of over forty, and a most respectable butler!' On 17 August 1875 specially struck silver RGS medals were distributed in Zanzibar to as many of the followers of Livingstone who were still alive as could be traced. They were inscribed with the words 'Faithful to the End', and Susi and Chuma were among the recipients.

While 'faithful' servants were made much of in England, the British ideal of the 'traditional servant attached to a mistress [or master] through bonds of fealty and vassalage' was already seen as a thing of the past, if it had ever really existed.

Even by the mid-eighteenth century, most servants had contracts. Indeed, as we have seen, most of Livingstone's servants were no more 'faithful' than their British counterparts and would change employment frequently without a second thought. Often, they were not even paid what they had been promised by the European explorers – Young records his regret at his calico supply getting spoiled *en route*, so that he was unable to fully honour his promises of payment to his followers. No wonder they often decided to go elsewhere for work. For example, in the Livingstone hagiography, much had always been made of his selfless dedication to his Kololo men and their devotion to him. But in fact, when Livingstone returned to reclaim his Kololo men, most had 'deserted' (or, in other words, chosen to do something else instead) and many more 'deserted' on their way back with him. Some decided that they did not want to go home at all. Even in the most imperialist of narratives, African decisions and choices sometimes peek through.

The fidelity of Susi and Chuma was probably not a servant's loyalty to their employer but perhaps more the deference and careful respect that attended the old and dying. In other words, Susi and Chuma were not *choosing* to remain faithful to Livingstone; they saw it as a matter of no choice. This explains their lack of any sense of having done anything exceptional, which puzzled Fraser. Their African sense of personhood was somewhat different from the individualist western version – and so models of 'servitude' or 'fidelity' do not translate in simple straightforward ways.

'Faithful to the End' presumably meant faithful to the end of *Livingstone's* life, but what happened to Susi and Chuma? They showed no anger at their treatment in Britain and vanished as quietly as they had come, as good servants should. By 20 October 1874 they were back in Zanzibar. According to Fraser, '[T]hey gradually sank into obscurity.' In fact, when Stanley returned to East Africa, he reported that Susi had 'fallen into very bad drinking habits, and was in a state of destitution through his debaucheries', although Stanley's racism must make us suspicious of his description of Africans. Anyway, by 1875 Susi was working again as a caravan leader for the UMCA. And Stanley took him on again to join him in his work for King Leopold II of Belgium in the Congo in 1879–82. From 1883 to 1891 Susi was a UMCA caravan leader, and he was baptised 'David' in August 1886. At some point he married, and he died in Zanzibar on 5 May 1891 of 'creeping paralysis', aged probably not much more than fifty. Chuma married the year after Livingstone's funeral and worked with the UMCA from 1875 to 1878. He turns up again in 1880, being presented with a sword and a silver medal in thanks for his headship of caravan of Joseph Thomson's RGS East African expedition. He worked on other expedition for Captain T. L. Phipson-Wybrants in 1880, and again for Thomson. He died of consumption in Zanzibar, still a young man of about thirty, in 1882.

But one thing is for sure – the Victorian idea that Africa existed in some kind of earlier stage of civilisation, and was immune to the 'modern', becomes utterly untenable if we take the trouble to think about the experience of these men. In some ways it could be argued that they were undergoing 'modernisation' at an even more terrifying rate than Anglo-Americans. This could obviously be painful – all of them seem to have encountered some difficulty once they returned to Africa, and we could cite the case of Livingstone's servant Sekwebu, whom Livingstone took with him on a steamer bound for England in 1856, but whose 'mind was affected' and who committed suicide by jumping overboard. 'We never found the body of poor Sekwebu,' Livingstone notes, wondering if it was the unfamiliarity of the ship and sea voyage that precipitated the man's traumatic demise. For those black servants that did make the voyage to England, the forced collision of different modernities must surely have been to some extent alarming, but perhaps less than we might like to think. The silence bequeathed to us does not necessarily denote frightened awe. European travellers did not find their encounters with African cultures so much alarming as surprising, complex and comic. Why should it be different the other way around? If we consider Livingstone's amused account of the African villagers 'bursting into uncontrollable laughter' when asked to kneel and pray to an unseen being, or Stanley's less amused account of being laughed at by Africans, which made him feel 'not much better than the monkey in the zoological collection at Central Park, whose funny antics elicit such bellows of laughter from young New Yorkers', it seems perfectly possible that these black men found cultural practices in Britain in 1874 equally hilarious. When Susi and Chuma left England, they left very little trace, but they had looked, and judged, and – worryingly for those like Stanley who believed in their innate inferiority – they might even have laughed.

In fact, some trace of Susi and Chuma's visit to Britain does survive to this day. On 12 August 1874 Horace Waller moved from Leytonstone to become Rector of Twywell Church in Northamptonshire, and Susi and Chuma came with him, staying in the little round tollhouse on the road into the village. Twywell was, and still is, a tiny rural community, and it is possible that Waller took the new position to give him more time for the editing of Livingstone's papers.

19. Carved pews in Twywell Church in Northamptonshire depicting chained slaves; Horace Waller (centre) and African elephants worshipping the cross.

It must have seemed an extraordinarily sleepy place to Susi and Chuma after London, and the big houses at Kelly and Newstead that they had visited. The honey-coloured stone church is quintessentially English – a beautiful example of twelfth-century Romanesque, tucked away behind the village, nestling in a grass churchyard. It is a surprise, then, to find the pews of the choir finely carved with scenes of African animals – including elephants worshipping the light of the Cross – and chained slaves being led to the light of Christ by Waller himself. A carving of Bishop Mackenzie's grave appears on the end of one of the pews. The pews were carved as a memorial to Waller after his death in 1896, and dedicated to his memory at a service in December 1898. The UMCA and the RGS both contributed to their cost. Susi and Chuma themselves are memorialised in a small glass display case in the church which contains their photographs and 'relics' of their visit. The case contains a miscellany of objects: the old keyring that used to hold the church key, thought to be made out of a piece of African wood possibly brought by Susi and Chuma from the tree under which they had buried Livingstone's heart; a piece of bark said to be preserved by the two servants from the wrapping of Livingstone's body on its journey from Chitambo's village to Zanzibar; a pair of 'native-made' pincers with which Mackenzie and Waller cut the shackles off the necks of slaves; and a reproduction of Waller's watercolour of Bishop Mackenzie's grave, the original of which hangs in the vestry. It is a curious little reliquary in a very Anglican context. There is one other photograph in the case too – it is of General Gordon, who stayed with the Wallers over Christmas 1879, bringing with him three stones from Calvary, which were placed behind the altar.

None of this tells us any more about what Susi and

Chuma made of England in 1874, but it does remind us that they were here and that a tiny corner of *this* foreign land will be forever Africa.

4

STANLEY

A meeting is, of course, always about two people, so what happened to Stanley after 1871? After Susi, Chuma and Wainwright's visits to Newstead, Augusta Fraser remembers that Stanley came to visit the Webb family in October 1872, just before he set off for his tour of lectures in America. One afternoon, they were all supposed to be going on a 'patriarchal walk' around the estate. The children were not keen on these walks, as 'they were always lengthy and much time was wasted, in our eyes, by dawdling about and standing over drains, fences, and other "improvements"'. So they were delighted when Stanley broke away from the party and set up a new game, 'an Exploring Expedition in Africa, to be led by himself'. He took the five children, aged six to fourteen, around the grounds:

> If they saw a fallen tree it was a terrible crocodile, a big stump a hippopotamus or an elephant, sheep and cows, antelopes or buffaloes; whilst even imaginary lions had not been wanting, and, of course, any stray folk they saw in the distance had been avoided as hostile tribes ... I never saw him look so boyish and happy as on this occasion. He was at his best with children, and most careful of them in all ways, gentle both in speech and manner.

20. Photograph of Stanley taken in Alexandria, Egypt when he was in his late twenties.

He had so much the heart of a boy hidden underneath
his manifold experiences, that he played, not with them,
but as one of themselves.

More than thirty years before Baden Powell published
Scouting for Boys in 1908, Stanley was already proving himself
an excellent scoutmaster; in fact, it is possible that the Boy
Scouts would never have been invented without Stanley.
In 1873 he published his only work of fiction – an adventure story for boys called *My Kalulu: Prince, King and Slave*.
It was generally agreed by its reviewers on both sides of the
Atlantic that the 'work is not one of much literary merit, but
it will doubtless prove interesting to the youthful readers
for whom it is ostensibly intended'. Stanley introduced the
book, saying, 'This book has been written for boys; not those
little darlings who are yet bothering over the alphabet, and
have to be taken to bed at sundown ... but for those clever,
bright-eyed, intelligent boys of all classes, who have begun to
be interested in romantic literature.' But while Stanley early
identified a potential youth market for his tales of derring-
do, he failed fully to exploit it himself. *My Kalulu* is rather a
ponderous read, full of archaic 'thees' and 'thous', as Stanley
tries to render the speech of his African characters, and the
book was not a great success. Nevertheless, his other travel
writing exerted an enormously important influence on *fin-
de-siècle* culture in Britain and America. This influence has
been largely forgotten because Stanley's shameful involvement with King Leopold's brutal regime in the Belgian
Congo led to his falling out of public favour when the truth
of the 'Congo Free State' was revealed in the early 1900s.
Nevertheless, Stanley's portrayal of 'darkest Africa' was so
popular and pervasive in the late nineteenth century that it

came to underpin much twentieth-century 'modern' thinking about primitivism and, indeed, modernism itself. Roger Fry, D. H. Lawrence, Conrad, Picasso and T. S. Eliot, to name but a few – exponents of western modernism drew inspiration from late Victorian accounts of Africa and collections of African objects.

In Britain, the Tories won the general election in 1874, the year of Livingstone's funeral, and stayed in power until 1880. Throughout these years, the government worked to create a myth of patriotism that was identified with conservatism, militarism and racialism: we have already seen how it attempted to use Livingstone's funeral to this end. With a similar Tory imperialist agenda, Queen Victoria was declared Empress of India in 1877 and the empire – possibly for the first time – began to come into sharper focus for more of the British people. The debate about democracy and what it meant to be a British citizen escalated at this time, and a concomitant anxiety about educating the youth of Britain for citizenship. Such anxieties were inflected through the myth of empire. This was not confined to the Tories: the Liberals too worried about inculcating patriotism in the young, without over-emphasising militarism and imperialism. Thinking about the ways in which Stanley's writing underpinned the development of Edwardian boys' fiction may start to help restore some of the complexity of his contribution to the history of the way the 'empire' was imagined.

It was in this increasingly conservative political climate that the Religious Tract Society set up the *Boy's Own Paper* in 1879. This was an illustrated boys' weekly, offering 'good, sound, lively reading' of a kind to make 'timid and weak-kneed boys brave, honest, and prosperous in life'. The *Boy's Own Paper* made boys feel important – as if they were central social actors and would grow up to have exciting adventures in a mythic country called 'the empire'. It promised further that these adventures would be not only exciting but – albeit vaguely – somehow essential to national security. One of the first issues ran a somewhat dutiful article on Livingstone, entitled 'The Life of a Missionary', which concentrated on self-sacrifice and religion, and was confined to two un-illustrated columns of dense text. 'Stanley's Adventures in Africa' offered an expurgated account of Stanley's recently published *Through the Dark Continent* (1878) – the account of his transcontinental African journey of 1874–7. Stanley's narrative was serialised over several weeks and lavishly illustrated with engravings from the book. It is clear which of the two explorers the editors considered more interesting to their boy readers. The extracts from *Through the Dark Continent* are bristling with aggression and made up largely of fight scenes. Faced with 'two hundred screaming black demons', Stanley is ready for action, telling his men, '"I have been ready these three hours. Are you ready, your guns and revolvers loaded, and your ears open this time?"' Later he reports exultantly, '"Four shots killed five men and sank two of the canoes."'

Along with Stanley, another of the paper's regular contributors was George A. Henty, who was, like Stanley, a newspaper journalist and war correspondent who published an amazing 103 volumes of adventure fiction between 1868 and 1902. Interviewed in the *Boy's Own Paper* in 1902, Henty said, 'I know that very many boys have joined the cadets and afterwards gone into the army through reading my stories.' Both Stanley's and Henty's narratives are deeply militaristic and insist on the pluckiness of the English boy in his encounter with the inferior races. Indeed, in 1873 Stanley had sailed with Henty out to the Gold Coast to cover the Asante campaign. Henty used episodes from his adventures with Stanley on the campaign in his adventure story *By Sheer Pluck*, making a boy called Swinburne, who was Stanley's valet and clerk, the hero of his story. Stanley himself never mentions this lad in his writings, just as he never mentioned William Hoffman, another of his personal servants, for whom he secured a job in Leopold's Congo and whom he later selected as a companion-servant on a trip to South Africa. He even left Hoffman £300 in his will, and Hoffman wrote after Stanley's death, 'I mite [*sic*] have been better off had I been wicked and earnt money, as some people wanted me to give some details of my late master, which will never be as I promised him it will go to my grave with me as Stanley was my dear beloved master and what I know is in my heart.'

In his autobiography, Stanley tells how he ran away, shocked, from a brothel and vomited when he smoked a cigar for the first time. He represents himself as innocent, even prudish. All that we know of Victorian workhouses and – even more definitely – of the merchant navy in the nineteenth century makes it unlikely that Stanley could have been as sexually innocent as he suggests. It is probable that he witnessed or was subjected to acts that would now be classified as rape or sexual abuse. Several of his biographers have noted a certain sexual ambivalence about Stanley, and it is true that he was awkward, even sullen, with women and seems to have been happiest in the company of younger men and boys – he travelled to Turkey in 1866 with the fifteen-year old Lewis Noe, passing him off as his 'half-brother'. In his exposé of Stanley in the *New York Sun* in August 1872, Noe described Stanley's sadistic pleasure when he 'stripped my clothing from my back, and on my bare skin scourged me with a whip which he cut from the trees, and on which he left the sharp knots, until the blood ran from my wounds. Stanley understands the refinement of cruelty in whipping.' Noe later threatened Stanley's widow with revealing 'everything' that happened on this trip and she was forced to pay him off. The other young man on the ill-fated Turkey trip, Harlow Cook, denied that Noe was telling the truth, however, and said Stanley had been 'basely slandered'. In 1866 Stanley asked if he could take one of the St Asaph's workhouse boys under his wing, but 'the boy's mother got wind of Stanley's intention and, becoming alarmed, refused her permission'. In 1869 Stanley made arrangements for the fourteen-year-old Edmund Balch to accompany him on a journey through Asia, but the boy's parents intervened, and he 'collected' Selim Heshmy, a young Christian Arab boy, in Jerusalem and the young slave boy Kalulu on his 1871 expedition to find Livingstone. Stanley enjoyed and sought out the company of boys and youths and he seems never to have entirely relinquished his own boyishness – a certain sense of being slightly at odds with the 'grown-up' world pervades his writing.

It is worth remembering that the Victorians were much more comfortable with eroticised male friendships than we are today. In a strange way their sexual vocabulary was wider than ours: our anxious identity politics force category distinctions between homosexual and heterosexual that one suspects might have seemed over-determined to many Victorian men.

In his public persona and in his writing, maybe Stanley transformed homoerotic feelings into a model of militaristic and homosocial masculinity that he connects with the bringing of civilisation and Christianity to dark places. Much has been written in recent years about Victorian ideas of masculinity and how they were either produced by or for a myth of empire. Stanley's version of masculinity was, perhaps, accidentally produced by empire, but was then reappropriated in the late Edwardian period to bolster faltering British confidence in the imperial idea. It is not at all clear that the idea of empire directly contributed to Stanley's version of manhood, or that Stanley's version of manhood directly contributed to the idea of empire: in fact, there was probably a complicated feedback loop between the two. The influence of the Victorian African experience on scouting continued. In 1895 Baden-Powell was sent out to raise a native force to attack the powerful Ashantis. After he pulled off the Livingstone story in 1872, Stanley, along with Henty, covered the first Ashanti Wars in what is now Ghana in West Africa. Baden-Powell would afterwards claim that much of his scouting lore was derived from the knowledge and customs of the warriors he engaged from the Krobos, Elima, Mumford and Adansi peoples.

In 1874 Stanley was back in London after his Ashanti experiences to attend Livingstone's funeral. That autumn the publisher John Murray wrote to Webb to ask if Stanley would be a suitable editor for Livingstone's *Last Journals*. Agnes Livingstone was very keen on the idea, as she liked and trusted Stanley. Webb's reply was interesting: 'I have little doubt but that his name being associated with the book would be popular with the public ... the question seems to displease the Geographers, or the British public ... The only question with regard to Stanley as Editor is will he forgo Americanisms and personalities?' Stanley was already gathering supplies for another expedition to Africa, anyway. On hearing of Livingstone's death, he had written, '[O]thers must go forward and fill the gap. "Close up, boys! Close up!"' In fact, as his African career unfolded, Stanley's boys' methods of opening up Africa proved to be much more brutal than Livingstone's. Nevertheless, Stanley's geographical achievements were considerable. On his next journey (1874–7), jointly sponsored by two newspapers, the *New York Herald* and the *Daily Telegraph*, he crossed the African continent, travelled more than 7,000 miles, and was the first European to track the course of the Congo and to solve the mystery of where it came from. The highly-coloured and action-packed newspaper reports he sent back did much to enrage groups such as the British and Foreign Anti-Slavery Society and the Aborgines' Protection Society, but the truth of Stanley's interaction with Africans is much more complex than has generally been acknowledged. In his new biography, *Stanley: the Impossible Life of Africa's Greatest Explorer*, Tim Jeal points out the extent to which a tradition of unfair and selective quotation has kept Stanley as the whipping boy of our post-colonial conscience. As an example he cites a much quoted passage in which Stanley calls his African servants 'slaves', and writes that, 'They are faithless, lying, thievish, indolent knaves, who only teach a man to despise himself for his folly in attempting a grand work with such miserable slaves.' Jeal adds that this quotation continues in Stanley's diary: '[s]lavery is abhorrent to my very soul, and all men engaged in the trade should be doomed to instant death, but these men make me regard myself every day as only a grade higher than a miserable slave driver.' Jeal points out that Stanley hated having to drive his men on, but it was done to save them and himself from giving up and slowly growing too weak to move through starvation. A few days later Stanley wrote that if he chose to abandon his men he would be able to save himself and about ten others but he could not bring himself to do that: 'Better by far to die as we have lived, together, and share fate even the most fearful. Yet my people anger me oh so much, and yet I pity and love them.' In the uncultivated parts of Africa giving up and stopping moving on a journey was a sure way to die – Stanley had to move his team on and he did punish them frequently – by putting them in slave chains, flogging them, threatening to shoot them and sometimes – on his last expedition – publicly hanging them as examples to their peers. But Jeal also shows that Stanley tended to exaggerate the violence of his expedition, often referring to brief and bloodless encounters as 'battles'. Presumably this was an attempt to engage his readers, serving up the kind of Africa he thought they expected, rather than describing the complexity of the country as he found it.

King Leopold II of Belgium had been reading about Stanley's progress across Africa from 1874 onwards with deep interest and had envoys ready to woo the explorer as soon as he stepped off the train in Paris on his way back from his triumphant transcontinental journey. Stanley was not interested at first, but when he had tried and failed to excite interest in Britain and America for his colonisation plans for the Congo basin area, he did cross to Belgium on 10 June 1878 to meet Leopold, and agreed to enter his service. It is unclear just how much Stanley initially understood of Leopold's true plans – which were not in fact for a colony but rather to make a private company of the Congo and the Congolese, in order ruthlessly to exploit the people and the land for his own personal gain. These plans were carefully disguised under a confusing series of 'philanthropic' organisations set up by Leopold, with which he even (briefly) managed

21. *Stanley attracted severe criticism for his methods of exploration in Africa: this is the frontispiece to D. J. Nicoll's 1890 exposé,* Stanley's Exploits: or Civilising Africa.

to hoodwink the Anti-Slavery Society and the Aborigines' Protection Society. In August 1879 Stanley went back to Africa as part of the newly established *Comité d'Études du Haut-Congo* (soon superseded by the *Association Internationale du Congo*) and it must have become clear to him at some point what the real plan was although he seems to have done his best to persuade himself that Leopold's work in Africa was altruistic and formed a fitting sequel to Livingstone's heroic attempts to bring Commerce, Christianity and Civilisation into Africa. Tim Jeal has shown how Stanley disagreed with Leopold taking land and sovereignty from Congolese chiefs and how Leopold ultimately employed a large team of treaty makers because Stanley refused to sign over African land for almost nothing to Leopold's private ownership: '[t]hese chiefs own and possess the soil,' he insisted. Stanley did, however, organise the building of roads across vast tracts of land in central Africa and established Belgian stations, but it is possible that he did this in good faith believing he was helping the Congolese. Certainly Jeal shows that almost all his closest colleagues and confidants at this time were black Africans. But one of Leopold's employees who later turned whistleblower, George Washington Williams, recorded the way in which Stanley's 'name produces a shudder among this simple folk when mentioned; they remember his broken promises, his copious profanity, his hot temper, his heavy blows, his severe and rigorous measures, by which they were mulcted of their lands'. The truth is hard to establish. Stanley was undoubtedly racist, but he may not have been as consistently vicious in his racism as he is later represented. Stanley returned from the Congo in 1884, and it is true that the worst of the atrocities happened after this date as industrialised countries began to increase their demands for more and more raw rubber which was obtained by forced labour in the Congo. Stanley's name would now be indelibly linked with the atrocities that flowed, but he was not in the Congo between 1890 and 1910 when the worst of the carnage happened.

When the carnage did happen, it was horrifying. African witness accounts were collected by Swahili-speaking agents, and they told of forced marches for days with no food or water, the old and sick being bayoneted to death and babies being thrown into the grass by the wayside to die. High-profile campaigners against these atrocities included a young British Consul Roger Casement, the campaigning journalist E. D. Morel and Arthur Conan Doyle – the creator of Sherlock Holmes. Conan Doyle had once been President of the Boys' Empire League and was a major force behind the re-efflorescence of Anglo-Saxonism at the King Alfred

Millenary in 1910, and an enthusiastic supporter of British policy in the Boer War, reminding us that being pro-Anglo-Saxon and pro-empire did not mean approving of *everything* that happened in Africa in the name of civilisation. But in fact it was the missionary societies back in Britain that really made the difference, and through the medium of photography. The missionary societies' photographic slide shows of mutilated Congolese bodies were the successor to the lantern slides that Livingstone had used to try and convert Africans. These graphic images caused a wave of popular disgust in Britain, and forced a political debate even before Roger Casement's exposé was published in 1904. In April 1884 the United States of America recognised the *Association Internationale du Congo*'s claim to the Congo. It was the first country to do so and this secured Leopold's position before the Berlin Conference kicked off in November that year. At the conference, conflicting claims on Africa were resolved so that West Africa, particularly the Congo and Niger rivers, could subsequently be sliced up in the so-called 'Scramble for Africa' and distributed between European nations greedy for a piece of the action. Stanley was delighted by America's official recognition, and he travelled back to Europe in the summer of 1884 in a very good mood, staying for a while with Leopold at his seaside villa in Ostend.

America may not have been an imperial power, but it had strong trading links with Africa: indeed, the first consul appointed to Zanzibar was a US representative who arrived in 1836. The British arrived five years later in 1841. It was America that was the first country to recognise the *Association Internationale du Congo* partly because of Leopold's promise to administer a free trade zone. At the Berlin Conference Stanley was both officially part of the American delegation and in the pay of Leopold. Leopold worked energetically behind the scenes with American contacts to keep Brussels in the loop when the big powers started to stake out Africa.

But at the 1884 Berlin Conference, a meeting about Africa at which not one African was present, the truth about Leopold's plans for the Congo was not widely known in Europe or America. In fact, Leopold's regime was weak and feeble at this time. In Berlin, Stanley acted as 'technical advisor' to the American delegation while he was still on Leopold's (generous) payroll. He enjoyed the association with royalty, and he dined with Bismarck, thoroughly savouring the social recognition for which he had been hungry for so long. But Leopold was not quite sure what to do with Stanley after the conference, perhaps realising that he lacked the kind of brutal racism against Africans necessary to finesse affairs in the Belgian Congo. It so happened that in 1886 the governor of the territory bordering on the Congo, equatorial Sudan, found himself under attack from a rebel Muslim fundamentalist movement, the Mahdists, and appealed for help from Europe. Despite his title, Emin Pasha, this governor was actually a German Jew and keen botanist called Eduard Schnitzer. Stanley was granted permission by Leopold to lead a relief expedition, on condition that he took a route through an unexplored region of the Congo and then added equatorial Sudan to Leopold's territory, with Emin as governor.

Perhaps because it was set to be another 'finding' by Stanley, the expedition attracted immense pre-publicity in Britain and America. In fact, it turned out to be nothing short of a disaster in ways that were not Stanley's fault. Stanley left Major Edmund Barttelot in charge of a rearguard, while he marched onward with a vanguard, most of which drowned or perished of disease on their way through the rainforest. Meanwhile, Barttelot seems to have lost his mind, decided he was being poisoned, and rampaged around killing and torturing Africans until he was finally shot by an African. Recognising the dramatic potential of this forgotten part of the story, a hundred years later Simon Gray was to write a play called *The Rear Column*, which was directed by Harold Pinter in London in 1978. By the time Stanley and the starving and weary remainder of his men made it through the forest, Emin Pasha actually rescued *them*, by providing essential food and supplies. Indeed, Emin Pasha was not now entirely sure that he wanted to be relieved, the rebel threat having eased if it had ever existed. Nor did he want to join his territory to Leopold's, or to negotiate with the British, and he did not in the end even accompany Stanley back to Europe. Nothing daunted, Stanley dramatised his encounter with Emin Pasha as another 'meeting' like his first famous meeting with Livingstone, and he wrote up the adventure in Cairo as *In Darkest Africa* (1890). Stanley was greeted as a popular hero upon his return to Britain in April 1890. The two volumes of *In Darkest Africa*, were 'read more universally and with deeper interest than any other publication [of 1890]'. The social reformer, William Booth, published *In Darkest England, and the way out* in 1890 in imitation of Stanley's famous title.

Some dissenting voices began to make themselves heard, and a rather different account of the expedition emerged with the posthumous publication of the diaries of one of the men Stanley had left waiting for orders and supplies for thirteen months. But despite Stanley's apparent abandonment of the rear column, many of whom perished without supplies, on the whole people in Britain and America did not

Meeting of Stanley & Emin Pasha at Kavalli on Lake Albert Nyanza

22. *A jigsaw puzzle of 1890. Stanley shakes Emin Pasha by the hand having 'found' him in a deliberate reprise of the iconic moment of his meeting with Livingstone.*

seem to notice the mismanagement of the expedition, and 1890 was – in many ways – Stanley's *annus mirabilis*. All sorts of commemorative products, including songs, poured forth once more, like 'The Victor's Return', with its rousing chorus which looked back to the Livingstone Relief Expedition: 'On, Stanley, on, were the words of yore: On, Stanley, on, let them ring once more ...' Indeed, the iconography of this meeting habitually leaned on the Livingstone meeting – Stanley is shown drinking champagne with Emin, just as he had done with Livingstone, or – even more frequently, as on a child's jigsaw puzzle of 1890, for example, shaking hands with

Emin Pasha in a jungle clearing. This is an image which also appeared on biscuit tins, scraps, tea caddies, plates and jugs. George Bernard Shaw groaned in 1890 that all society had succumbed to 'Stanley worship'.

By this time, 'Mr H. M. Stanley' was enjoying life as a commodity in Britain, too, endorsing Victor Vaissier's CONGO SOAP in an advertisement which shows a grey-haired but rugged Stanley in a hat that looks much like Livingstone's famous consular cap – surely not coincidentally. Stanley is carrying a large box of soap strung on a pole over his shoulder; 'I consider the soap excellent,' he says. He also endorsed Keble's pipes and Edgington tents, and advertisements appeared using Stanley and Africa for the United Kingdom Tea Company, Bovril and Pears' soap. But the same British public hardly noticed when, two years later, Emin Pasha – having returned to exactly the territory that Stanley was supposed to have 'rescued' him from – was decapitated with a machete in the Ituri Forest, as a final confirmation of the absurdity of Stanley's costly mission. Nobody noticed because, unlike in 1872, when they had been fascinated by the idea of Livingstone, this time round they could not really care less about Emin Pasha: all eyes were on Stanley and the resonance of the adventure was all in the echo of the Livingstone Search & Relief Expedition.

To crown it all, 1890 was also the year in which the *Stanley and African Exhibition* opened on London's Regent Street. While the catalogue boasted that it would 'bring the conditions of life in Africa more clearly before the visitor's mind', the exhibition really served only to recycle and reinforce every possible prejudice and cliché about 'darkest Africa'. Despite its unashamedly popular appeal – the visitors approached the exhibition, for example, through the 'gate

23. A display case from the Stanley and African Exhibition of 1890 showing African objects arranged decoratively as trophies with no attempt at context or explanation.

of village palisade ornamented with skulls. <u>EN ROUTE</u> FOR THE HEART OF SAVAGE AFRICA', as if they were entering a fairground ride – the list of patrons reads like a 'who's who' of the geographic establishment. Of the seventy-seven names on the list, many, such as William Webb, had always been reasonably well disposed to Stanley, but others, such as Richard Burton and John Kirk, were the very people who had spurned him twenty years before. Stanley had clearly been gaining ground with the gentleman geographers and had also succeeded in identifying himself as part of the British establishment. African objects lent by the Anti-Slavery Society and the Church Missionary Society were being displayed alongside exhibits lent by 'His Majesty the King of the Belgians, from the Congo State Collection'. After the skulls, the visitor would encounter a bust of Stanley in the vestibule, and then two further portraits of him in the dome, along with a portrait of the Queen and one of Leopold. In the centre of the exhibition hall was another bust of Stanley. The exhibition was otherwise crowded with African objects which were listed in the catalogue with no context or explanation whatsoever, so how clearly African life *was* actually brought before the visitor's mind is debatable. Really what was brought before the visitor's mind, apart from Stanley's visage – several times over – was the heroic myth of British exploration in Africa, which is rather a different thing when you think about it. In the 'Explorers' Section', for example, Case One contained 'Relics of Dr Livingstone', including his consular cap and his teaspoons. There was also a tearoom and various souvenirs were on sale, such as a commemorative photograph of the two little African boys who were on display as a 'live' exhibit. The Anti-Slavery Society later took their 'owners', a couple called the Thorburns, to the High Court on charges of cruelty to the boys. But the exhibition claimed to offer a jolly good day out for all the family.

And finally 1890 was the year in which, on 12 July in Westminster Abbey, Stanley married Dorothy Tennant, a British artist who also had an interest in boys – her hallmark was the sentimental depiction of plucky 'ragamuffins' and street children. She later illustrated editions of Stanley's work with little designs of 'picaninnies' at the chapter ends. Marrying one another seems to have rather surprised both of them. Stanley was forty-nine and Tennant was thirty-six. The couple ordered an extravagant wreath to be laid on Livingstone's grave during their wedding service: Stanley was always anxious that his name continued to be linked with Livingstone's in the public mind. When Stanley himself died in 1904, the *Times* obituary compared the two men: 'Physically, like most great African explorers, [Stanley] was of small stature, with a strongly marked dark brown face, keen eyes, and powerful jaw, wonderfully like Livingstone's.' In fact, photographs show that the two men were not physically similar at all.

Dorothy, who enjoyed her new-found status as the wife of a famous man, became an attentive partner, although Stanley's young male assistant accompanied them on their honeymoon and on all their subsequent lecture tours. After his marriage, and when he had recovered from the acute gastritis that had afflicted him on his wedding day, Stanley capitalised on both his fame and his notoriety by giving a lecture tour in America, travelling around in a specially customised Pullman car with 'Henry Morton Stanley' emblazoned on the side, and then a tour in Britain, and another in 1891 in Australia and New Zealand. In 1896 the couple adopted a baby boy, Denzil, from relatives of Stanley's in North Wales. Stanley was touchingly soppy about the boy, writing to Dorothy when he was away from home, '[L]ook where I may, his beautiful features, lightened up with a sunny smile, come before my eyes all the time!' Despite Stanley's affection for America, the Stanleys settled in Britain and in 1898

Stanley bought a large mock-Tudor house called Furze Hill, in Pirbright, Surrey. Dorothy named a small wood in the grounds the 'Aruwimi Forest', a stream in the garden 'the Congo'and a pond 'Stanley Pool'.

She reproduced a miniature Africa in their Surrey garden partly in an attempt to prevent Stanley from ever going back to the 'dark continent' itself. Instead, she insisted that he stood for Parliament in Britain. To do this, he had quietly to transfer his citizenship from America to England. His first attempt at electioneering was hardly a great success. He was jeered off the platform in Lambeth North and lost to the Radicals. But – mainly due to his wife's dogged work on his behalf – he won the seat for the Liberal Unionists at the next general election in July 1895. Stanley was unenthusiastic about life as an MP: ever the impatient and self-directed man of action, he found 'degradation' in the 'servitude' required. He was bored, complaining that in the House, '[W]e listened to the most dreary twaddle it has ever been my lot to hear', and he felt the science of government was better managed in America.

Stanley's party, the Unionists, was against Home Rule for Ireland, and – on the whole – pro-empire, as Stanley continued to be until his death. But it is worth noting that Stanley was not a conservative, and his politics were never straightforwardly Tory. He never returned to explore in Africa, although he did tour South Africa in 1897 in the company of the faithful Hoffman. He never wavered in his support of the Boer War, but he was rumoured to be unhappy about the revelations coming out of the Congo at the end of the century about Leopold's regime, and wrote privately of Leopold's 'erring and ignorant policy'. It is difficult to gauge his true view, as he never spoke publicly about the Congo, and his contribution to parliamentary debates – even on colonial subjects – was minimal. He did publish a revealing article entitled 'Anglo-Saxon Responsibilities' in September 1899 in an American periodical, *The Outlook*. After a long attack on Gladstone's 'peace-at-any-price' policies, which he dubs the 'Gladstonian sickness', he extols the virtues of imperialism, and announces that 'experience proves that as a race we are fitter for these responsibilities than any other'. Stanley's article came out at the same time as Kipling's famous poem 'The White Men's Burden' and both were directed towards America and the recent US conquest of the Philippines and other former Spanish colonies. Stanley's article is also addressed from Britain to America and ends:

> We cannot accuse you, nor can you accuse us, of earth-hunger or of common, sordid motives, but we have listened to the plaints of injured and oppressed peoples in Burmah, Egypt, Uganda, Benin, Ashantee, Nyassa, Matabele, and a score of other places, and as you in Cuba, Porto Rico, and the Philippines did; and as we have done towards our suppliants, so you will do to yours, viz., work with them and by them for their own welfare, progress, and interest. And it may be that we shall both be called to do the same again, and, please God, we shall do our duty; but our duty will be smoother and easier if we know that we have one another's sympathy.

It is a justification of Anglo-American imperialism that we are still hearing today.

One striking fact remains: Stanley's close friendship with an American called Samuel L. Clemens, a.k.a. Mark Twain, continued to the end of his life. Twain introduced Stanley's

Boston lecture in November 1886, and the two corresponded right up to 1904, the year of Stanley's death. Twain was one of the fiercest and most outspoken opponents in America of the Boer War and of Leopold's Congo: he published the devastating satire *King Leopold's Soliloquy: A Defense of his Congo Rule* in 1905, with all proceeds going to the Congo Reform Association. But he also said about his friend Stanley, seemingly without a shred of irony, '[w]hen you compare these achievements of his with the achievements of really great men who exist in history, the comparison, I believe, is in his favour.' Twain also, of course, wrote brilliantly about boys and their adventures, and perhaps it was Stanley's boyishness that kept their friendship warm, despite political differences. But the friendship is also a strong indication that Stanley was not the monster he was later taken to be. In 1899 Stanley was knighted by the Tory government, before the Congo scandal really broke. On 9 May 1904, after a year of incapacity after a severe stroke, Stanley, 'the exuberant American', died at his London flat in Richmond Terrace. In February of that same year, Roger Casement's official report on the Congo had been published and had caused shockwaves throughout the government and beyond, and consequently Stanley's heroic reputation was melting fast, so fast that the Dean of Westminster Abbey felt unable to allow his burial in the abbey that year. So Stanley did not finally rest next to Livingstone, as he had wished. Instead, his ashes were buried in the village churchyard at Pirbright.

What do boys represent in this story, then? A certain kind of plucky against-the-odds optimism, self-reliance and the victory of the 'little man' over the establishment, of course. But the fantasy of the boy also allows for an innocence – a childish lack of responsibility of just the kind that Stanley was always imagining Africans displayed, and was always criticising them for. The 'dusky children of Ethiop' may need looking after, but the empire boys want to be children too – playing what Kipling in his empire-boy novel *Kim* calls the 'Great Game'. In the Preface to *My Kalulu*, Stanley reveals that, as far as he is concerned, the category of 'boy' is not an age-specific one: 'For those boys, and young, middle-aged, and old men, who found my first book rather heavy, I beg to offer something lighter, fresher – a romance.' The empire could be imagined as a place without consequences – a kind of fantasy space of 'romance' that had no connection what-soever with the 'civilised' world.

STANLEY'S EARLY LIFE AS JOHN ROWLANDS

Stanley travelled an immense distance during his life, in miles but also in status, nationality, occupation, class and almost everything else. His curriculum vitae is striking as an example of nineteenth-century social and geographical mobility. Dumped in a workhouse in North Wales at the age of six, he never knew his father, but was reconciled later in life with his mother. Discharged from the workhouse on 13 May 1854, his first job was as a pupil-schoolmaster in North Wales; then he was a shop boy in a haberdasher's in Liverpool; a butcher's boy in Liverpool; a cabin boy on an American ship; an American store boy; a paid nurse in New Orleans; a store clerk in Arkansas; a Confederate soldier; a prisoner of war; a Union soldier; an attorney's clerk in New York; a ship's clerk in the federal fleet; an agricultural labourer; a hand on an oyster schooner; a war correspondent; an African explorer; an imperialist; and finally the British Liberal Unionist MP for Lambeth North. His extraordinary and highly fictionalised autobiography was left unfinished at his death, and was edited and published by his widow, Dorothy, in 1909. It hardly qualifies as a reliable account, but its inventions are themselves revealing of Stanley's need to fantasise an appropriate origin for the famous man he had become. Even the obituary which appeared in *The Times* on 11 May 1904 prickles with uncertainty about the details of Stanley's early life, qualifying many of its details with 'it seems', 'it is said', 'it is believed' and so on. 'A lady of undoubted veracity' who knew the young Rowlands in New Orleans in 1859 recalled him as 'always a boy of good habits, smart as a whip, and much given to bragging, big talk and telling stories'.

Stanley seems to have led a hand-to-mouth existence, working alongside what he calls the 'sooty-faced nigger[s]' on Southern plantations until the Civil War, when he enlisted for the Confederacy, was taken prisoner by the Union side and ended up fighting for the North instead. He felt 'a secret scorn for people who could kill one another for the sake of African slaves. There were no blackies in Wales, so why a sooty-faced nigger from a distant land should be an element of disturbance between white brothers, was a puzzle to me.' Finally, he deserted and went off to make his fortune in the Wild West, where he started selling colourful articles to the papers. He travelled to Turkey with Noe and Cook, and when he returned to America, Stanley was promoted by the *Missouri Democrat* and made special correspondent to cover Major-General Winfield Scott Hancock's peace-making expedition to the Plains Indians, the Cheyenne and the Sioux, in Kansas and Nebraska. His highly colourful accounts of the 'Indian Wars' impressed James Gordon Bennett Sr, the proprietor of the *New York Herald*. Stanley was to prove a perfect match for the *Herald* – the journalist who had no nation and no particular allegiance to anyone would suit the paper of which one contemporary observer remarked, 'No one has any idea what it stands for; to tell the truth, one suspects it doesn't have any fixed principles ... it knows only that it is for the winning side.'

In 1862 Stanley made his first big splash. He went free-lance to cover the Abyssinian Campaign, with an agreement to sell his stories first to the *Herald*, and he was determined to win the race to file the first story. George Macdonald Fraser has pastiched this campaign in *Flashman on the March* (2005) in which 'Sir Harry Flashman, V.C., arch-cad, poltroon, amorist, and reluctant hero' gets entangled in the campaign to free the Britons held hostage by King Tewodros (often called Theodore in the Anglo-American press), who imagined himself slighted by Queen Victoria. The Flashman stories are grounded in the kind of Victorian heroic rhetoric of empire that Stanley was later to produce by the yard. Like Flashman, Stanley was enough of a 'cad' to gain an advantage early in the race – he stopped at Suez, where the cable connection to New York ended, and befriended the chief telegraphist, tipping him generously to ensure that his dispatches would get through first when the time came. He was caught in the thick of the battle at the fort of Magdala, but the hardest part for Stanley was getting the story back to the coast through a flood in which his mule drowned. He did it by the skin of his teeth and smuggled the story off his ship while he was quarantined at Suez. His bribe paid off, and he beat the British press to its own story. In fact, he beat the British by several days, because just after his stories had been dispatched, the underwater cable broke – not even Stanley could have arranged this. Stanley's version was colourful and action-packed: 'No mercy was asked ... no puny blows were dealt; heads were chopped off, arms and limbs severed from trunks, and dead man lay stark and stiff plentifully. But they were all Abyssinians.' The *Herald* was first accused of inventing news and then gloriously exonerated when the official messages from General Sir Robert Napier finally reached London. Stanley was immediately appointed to the *Herald*'s permanent staff as a roving foreign correspondent. 'I must keep a sharp look out that my second coup shall be as much a success as the first,' he wrote. Of course, his second coup – finding Livingstone – would be even more successful, but it would be subject to the same suspicions as the first, as we have seen.

STANLEY'S LEGACY

Because the growing unease about Stanley's methods in Africa began to cloud his reputation at the end of the nineteenth century, he has not been the object of such enduring interest as Livingstone. This is a distortion of history of a kind, though. In fact it was Stanley who ensured Livingstone's fame, and Stanley who was the more famous on both sides of the Atlantic at the end of the nineteenth century. But while Livingstone's statue still stands on the edge of Victoria Falls, Stanley's legacy in Africa is besmirched by the atrocities of the Congo Free State. In 2004 the South African photographer Guy Tillim exhibited a series of photographs called *Leopold and Mobutu* around the world. He took the photographs in the Congo. One of the images shows the discarded, mutilated and dumped statue of Stanley lying face down on a rusting steamboat. The statue was removed during the Mobutu period of Africanisation in the 1970s and dumped in a government transport lot in Kinshasa. Stanley may have been discredited, and – partly because of this – his immense influence on Anglo-American culture from the 1870s onwards has never fully been considered. By 1890 both Britain and America couldn't get enough of him, and it is worthwhile trying to work out why.

There is one place where Stanley is still remembered with affection and gratitude: Belgium. Many of Stanley's papers were given or sold to the Musée Royal de l'Afrique Centrale by his adopted son in the 1950s. In 1991 the museum mounted an exhibition called *H. M. Stanley, Explorateur au Service du Roi*, and the catalogue is still on sale at the museum. The introduction by the museum's then director looks back to the glory days of the Belgian Congo:

> Cette présence belge au centre de l'Afrique était due, presqu'exclusivement, à l'initiative d'un seul homme, le Roi Léopold II, qui désirait étendre au-delà des mers les perspectives de son petit pays. Mais la réalisation d'un tel projet et l'aménagement de ce territoire africain n'auraient pu être menés à bien sans l'indispensable collaboration, sur place, d'un organisateur: l'explorateur H. M. Stanley.

> [This Belgian presence in Central Africa was almost entirely the result of the initiative of a single man, King Leopold II, who wanted to extend the reach of his small country overseas. But the realisation of such a project and the running of the African territory could not have been achieved without the invaluable collaboration on site of a manager: the explorer, H. M. Stanley.]

The account which follows of Stanley's role in the Congo

makes no reference to the scandal of the early 1900s, and maintains a hushed and reverent tone towards Leopold. In the preface to his 1989 biography of Stanley, Frank McLynn complained that 'the museum's administrators pursue a policy of turning away all parties interested in inspecting the original documentation [on Stanley]'. Today, the museum's website admits that 'The permanent exhibition has hardly changed since the nineteen-sixties. It still reflects the European colonial view of Africa at that time. The Museum has to be modern and dynamic. Therefore the form and content of the exhibition galleries must be urgently renovated.' Some modernisation is already afoot: a new café serving African food has apparently been a success, for example, and scholars are now being given access to the archives. But the museum is still a long way from becoming fully reflective about its own past, and perhaps for this very reason it remains disturbing and intriguing as a kind of museum of a museum.

Even the Musée Royal de l'Afrique Centrale has decided it has to get rid of the 'European colonial view of Africa'. But whether we like it or not – and most likely we do not – the European colonial view formed our modern world. Of course we should distance ourselves from the colonial past, but we cannot lose sight of it – lest we forget that men like Stanley created myths about 'the dark continent' that have not yet lost their power. The impact of Stanley on modern – and particularly on modernist – culture has never been properly recognised. Despite his lack of engagement with Africans, Stanley's writings were hugely important to creating a myth of primitive Africa which has stayed with us to this day. Joseph Conrad's *Heart of Darkness* (1899) owes much not only to his reading of Livingstone as a youth, but also to his reading of Stanley's accounts of Livingstone.

The book certainly imitates the urgent quest narrative of Stanley's *How I Found Livingstone* as Marlow pushes into the 'interior' to find Kurtz. 'Neither will the monuments left by all sorts of empire builders suppress for me the memory of David Livingstone,' wrote Conrad, 'the most venerated perhaps of all the objects of my early geographical enthusiasm.' It is a characteristically evasive remark – by refusing to connect Livingstone with imperialism, Conrad can have it both ways, celebrating the glory days of exploration while distancing himself from the 'empire builders'.

The American Edgar Rice Burroughs claimed that he wrote the first of his celebrated Tarzan books in 1912 with the aid of 'a 50-cent Sears dictionary and Stanley's *In Darkest Africa*'. The Tarzan series was immediately immensely popular and has remained so – spawning more than forty films, including a 1999 Disney version. For good or bad, Stanley's version of Africa still circulates in the global unconscious today. And in a very powerful way Stanley has always been part of that unconscious. He lurks in psychoanalytic theory and behind modern concepts of identity. Sigmund Freud read Stanley avidly in his youth, and he went on to make clear connections between the female and the primitive, as when he compares the female psyche to a 'dark continent' in Stanley's own phrase. The very basis of our modern thinking about ourselves incorporates some of Stanley's Africa.

Walter Benjamin suggested, 'History decomposes into images, not narratives', and Livingstone and Stanley's history has decomposed so fully that all we are left with is the image of two men clasping hands in the jungle. The representation of that meeting in 1871 has recirculated in political cartoons in English-language newspapers up to this day.

The meeting between Livingstone and Stanley is a reliable image that the press itself made famous and therefore continued to call upon. Many of these cartoons show two white men alone deep in the jungle. Sometimes Stanley's subsequent career in the Congo is elided with the Livingstone meeting, as in a cartoon by Yardley published in the *New York Times* on 30 April 1962, entitled 'Dr Adoula, I presume?', where the meeting takes place in the Congo. Clearly by now 'Stanley and Livingstone' have come to signify 'Africa' in a vague and generic way.

Peter Brookes's 1998 cartoon in *The Times* actually uses the original *Illustrated London News* print of the Stanley–Livingstone meeting, but makes some significant changes. Dr Livingstone has become the left-wing London mayoral candidate, his namesake Ken Livingstone, a.k.a. Red Ken. The black Africans behind the Livingstone character are given placards to hold emblazoned with slogans such as 'Ethnic lesbian politically correct trade unionists for Ken'. The cartoon seems to be reinscribing racism in one of its late-twentieth-century formations as anti-political correctness. Perhaps unsurprisingly, given the happy coincidence in their surnames, Brookes can't resist using the same joke again four years later. This time Tony Blair is on his 2002 Africa tour and encounters black Africans with banners reading 'Keep public services public!' and so on. What is striking about the earlier cartoon, though, is its circulation of the original 1872 image – a recirculation that keeps this meeting static and iconic. Brookes's cartoons do not require their audience to think beyond recognising that the black characters are black. They do not encourage any reconsideration or reflection on the Stanley and Livingstone myth. The moment remains tightly packed and impenetrable – a reference to a story that still resonates vaguely, even though its substance has all but disappeared.

Or has it? While much of the historical context of the meeting has been emptied out, Stanley's Africa continues to circulate in our culture in powerful and often unacknowledged ways. The history we construct for ourselves is made as much from what we forget as from what we remember. All sorts of things have to be forgotten and repressed in making heroes. But if we shield our eyes from the heroes for a while their surroundings come back into view and remind us that the global history of modernity is much more complicated than we like to think.

FURTHER READING

The literature on Livingstone and Stanley is huge, and I have read much more of it than I have space to list here. These notes will cite only the most significant texts used in each chapter.

Generally, Tim Jeal's classic biography *Livingstone* (1973) is indispensable, and was a constant point of reference throughout. I also read the two classic nineteenth-century biographies: William Garden Blaikie, *The Personal Life of David Livingstone* (1880) and Thomas Hughes, *David Livingstone* (1889). In addition to *The Autobiography of Sir Henry Morton Stanley* edited Dorothy Stanley (1909), I used several biographies of Stanley: John Bierman, *Dark Safari: The Life Behind the Legend of Henry Morton Stanley* (1990); Frank McLynn, *Stanley: The Making of an African Explorer* (1989); Richard Hall, *Stanley: An Adventurer Explored* (1974); and Ian I. Anstruther, *I Presume: Stanley's Triumph and Disaster* (1956). Other books critical to my research were *David Livingstone and the Victorian Encounter with Africa* (1996), the catalogue of an exhibition held at the National Portrait Gallery, London, from 22 March to 7 July 1996, and at the Scottish NPG, Edinburgh, from 26 July to 6 October 1996, and Felix Driver's excellent *Geography Militant: Cultures of Exploration and Empire* (2001). Tim Young's book, *Travellers in Africa: British Travelogue 1850–*

1900 (1994) and James Ryan's *Picturing Empire: Photography and the Visualisation of the British Empire* (1997) were also helpful. Adam Hochschild's *King Leopold's Ghost: A Tale of Greed, Terror, and Heroism in Colonial Africa* (1999) was useful for Chapter 4, but more generally provided an outstanding example of how popular history should be written.

Bibliographies of Livingstone material include James A. Casada, *Dr. David Livingstone & Sir Henry Morton Stanley: An Annotated Bibliography* (1976) and G. W. Clendennen and I. C. Cunningham, *David Livingstone: A Catalogue of Documents* (National Library of Scotland, 1979) and *Supplement* (1985).

The on-line resources I used most often include the Times Digital Archive, the American Memory website (Library of Congress) at http://memory.loc.gov/ammem/index.html and the Mellon-funded Making of America site at http://www.hti.umich.edu/m/moagrp/, the Oxford Dictionary of National Biography, the Royal Historical Society Bibliography at http://www.rhs.ac.uk/bibl/, the Royal Geographical Society Archive at http://www.rgs.org/ and the Livingstone Project, based at University College London and sponsored by the Wellcome Trust, which has a website on Livingstone's medical writings at www.livingstoneonline.ucl.ac.uk.

INTRODUCTION

In writing this introduction I have used Henry M. Stanley, *How I Found Livingstone. Travels, Adventures, and Discoveries in Central America; Including Four Month's Residence with Mr. Livingstone. By Henry M. Stanley, Travelling Correspondent of the 'New York Herald'* (1872) and E. D. Young, *The Search After Livingstone [A Diary Kept During the Investigation of his Reported Murder]* (1868). I also referred to a wide variety of popular biographies of Livingstone published throughout the twentieth century, including *David Livingstone: Heroic Missionary, Intrepid Explorer and the Black Man's Friend* (1928), which is quoted here. Also useful were Andrew Ross, *David Livingstone: Mission and Empire* (2002), and David Gilmour's review of it, 'The Great Victorian Abroad', in the *New York Review of Books*, 23 June 2005, pp. 28–30; Dorothy O. Helly, *Livingstone's Legacy: Horace Waller and Victorian Mythmaking* (1987); Andrew Porter, *Religion versus Empire? British Protestant Missionaries and Overseas Expansion, 1700–1914* (2004); and Timothy Holmes, *Journey to Livingstone: Exploration of an Imperial Myth* (1993). Newspapers I have used are the *Illustrated London News, The Times* and the *New York Herald*.

1 LIVINGSTONE

I have made extensive use of Livingstone's own writings and letters in my discussion of his career up to 1871. Most important is David Livingstone, *Missionary Travels and Researches in South Africa; including a sketch of Sixteen Years' Residence in the Interior of Africa, and a Journey from the Cape of Good Hope to Loanda on the West Coast; Thence across the Continent, Down the River Zambesi, to the Eastern Ocean* (1857), but also David and Charles Livingstone, *Narrative of an Expedition to the Zambesi and its Tributaries: and of the Discovery of the Lakes Shirwa and Nyassa: 1858–1864* (1865); *Dr Livingstone's Cambridge Lectures* (1860); *David Livingstone: Letters & Documents, 1841–1872: The Zambian collection at the Livingstone Museum*, edited by Timothy Holmes (1990); *Family Letters, 1841–1856: David Livingstone*, edited by I. Schapera (1959); Livingstone, 'Transvaal Boers' (1853); and MS letters from the collection of Quentin Keynes.

Other major references are J. M. MacKenzie, 'On Scotland and the Empire', *International History Review*, xv, 4 (1993): 714–39; *The Last Journals of David Livingstone in Central Africa, from 1865 to his Death: Continued by a Narrative of his Last Moments and Sufferings, Obtained from his Faithful Servants, Chuma and Susi*, edited by Horace Waller (1874); A. Z. Fraser (a.k.a. Alice Spinner), *Livingstone and Newstead* (1913); and J. M. MacKenzie, 'David Livingstone, The Construction of the Myth' in *Sermons and Battle Hymns: Protestant Popular Culture in Modern Scotland*, edited by G. Walker and T. Gallagher (1991). Richard Altick lists *Missionary Travels* as a bigger bestseller than Macaulay's *History* in *The English Common Reader: A Social History of the Mass Reading Public, 1800–1900* (1957) and I also consulted J. Henry Harper, *The House of Harper: A Century of Publishing in Franklin Square* (1912), for details of its American publication. Studies of Mary Livingstone include Margaret Forster, *Good Wives?: Mary, Fanny, Jennie and Me, 1845–2001* (2002) and Edna Healey, *Wives of Fame: Mary Livingstone, Jenny Marx, Emma Darwin* (1986).

The debate over nineteenth-century British attitudes to empire can be traced in the works of J. M. MacKenzie, *Propaganda and Empire: The Manipulation of British Public Opinion, 1880–1960* (1984); Catherine Hall, *Civilising Subjects: Metropole and Colony in the English Imagination, 1830–1867* (2002); and Bernard Porter, *The Absent-minded Imperialists: Empire, Society, and Culture in Britain* (2004). See also Chris Bayly's wonderful *The Birth of Modern World 1780–1914: Global Connections and Comparisons* (2004).

On the press in the nineteenth century, I consulted Alan J. Lee, *The Origins of the Popular Press 1855–1914* (1976); Lucy Brown, *Victorian News and Newspapers* (1985); Michael Emery, Edwin Emery and Nancy L. Roberts, *The Press in America: An*

Interpretive History of the Mass Media (2000); Mark Wahlgren Summers, *The Press Gang: Newspapers and Politics 1865–1878* (1994); William E. Huntzicker, *The Popular Press 1833–1865* (1999); Menahem Blondheim, *News Over the Wires: The Telegraph and the Flow of Public Information in America 1844–1897* (1994); and Hazel Dickens-Garcia, *Journalistic Standards in Nineteenth-Century America* (1989).

Carus Farrar's Narrative is reprinted in H. B. Thomas, 'The Death of Dr. Livingtone: Carus Farrar's Narrative', *Uganda Journal*, 14, 2 (September 1950): 115–28.

For more on the African experience of imperialism, see Isabel Hofmeyr, *We Spend Our Days as a Tale That is Told: Oral Historical Narrative in a South African Chiefdom* (1993); Paul Landau, *The Realm of the Word: Language, Gender, and Christianity in a Southern African Kingdom* (1995); and Birgit Meyers, *Translating the Devil: Religion and Modernity among the Ewe in Ghana* (1999). I also referred to Andrew Porter, 'The Universities' Mission to Central Africa': Anglo-Catholicism and the Twentieth-century Colonial Encounter', in *Missions, Nationalism, and the End of Empire*, edited by Brian Stanley and Alaine Low (2003), and his 'Commerce and Christianity: The Rise and Fall of a Nineteenth-Century Missionary Slogan', *Historical Journal*, xxviii (1985): 597–621; and Derek Peterson, *Creative Writing: Translation, Book-keeping, and the Work of Imagination in Colonial Kenya* (2004) and Adrian Hastings, *The Church in Africa: 1450–1950* (1994).

Other texts referred to in this chapter are H. G. Wells, *Experiment in Autobiography* (1934); *Madame Tussaud and Sons Waxwork Museum Catalogue* (1873); Lieutenant-General R. S. S. Baden-Powell, *Scouting for Boys: A Handbook for Instruction in Good Citizenship* (1908), originally printed in fortnightly parts at 4d each; Dean Rapp and Charles W. Weber, 'British

Film, Empire and Society in the Twenties: The "Livingstone" film, 1923–1925', *Historical Journal of Film, Radio and Television*, 9, 1 (1989): 3–17; *Handbook of the David Livingstone Memorial Museum*, compiled by W. V. Brelsford, District Officer (Rhodes-Livingstone Institute, Northern Rhodesia, 1937); Peter J. Westwood, *David Livingstone: His Life and Work as Told through the Media of Postage Stamps and Allied Material* (1986); *Festival of Britain: Preview and Guide (Daily Mail* Publication, 1951); Becky E. Conekin, *'The Autobiography of a Nation': The 1951 Festival of Britain* (2003); *The Fifth Reader, The School Board Readers, Adapted to the Requirements of the New Code* (1871); Stephen Heathorn, *For Home, Country, and Race: Constructing Gender, Class, and Englishness in the Elementary School 1880–1914* (2000); Valerie E. Chancellor, *History for their Masters. Opinion in the English Textbook, 1800–1914* (1970); James I. Macnair, *The Story of the Scottish National Memorial to David Livingstone* (1929); Max Jones, *The Last Great Quest: Captain Scott's Antarctic Sacrifice* (2003); Judith Listowel, *The Other Livingstone* (1974); and Oliver Ransford, *David Livingstone: The Dark Interior* (1978).

Modern rewritings of the Livingstone story include Ngugi Wa Thiong'o, *The River Between* (1965); Nadine Gordimer, *Livingstone's Companions: Stories* (1972); Marlene Nourbese Philip, *Looking for Livingstone: An Odyssey of Silence* (1991); Barbara Kingsolver, *The Poisonwood Bible* (1998); Pagan Kennedy, *Black Livingstone: A True Tale of Adventure in the Nineteenth-Century Congo* (2002); Martin Dugard, *Into Africa: The Epic Adventures of Stanley and Livingstone* (2003); and Robin Wayne Bailey, 'The Terminal Solution', in *ReVisions*, edited by Julie E. Czerneda and Isaac Szpindel (2004).

Newspapers and periodicals I have used are the *Illustrated London News, The Times, Boy's Own Paper, Radio Times* and the *Leisure Hour*.

2 THE MEETING

Jeal includes an appendix to his biography of Livingstone called 'The Date of the Stanley–Livingstone Meeting' in which he speculates that the meeting probably happened some time between 3 and 18 November 1871. Elizabeth Isichei describes Ujiji in the nineteenth century thus: 'Its buildings mirrored the encounter of cultures, for they "represented almost every style of African architecture – the huge-roofed Indian bungalow, the flat roofed tembe, the quadrangular hut of the Waswahili with baraza in front, and the beehive-shaped hut of most of the natives."' (*A History of African Societies to 1870*, 1997). The quote about the African in the opera hat comes from Henry Walton, *Livingstone Fifty Years After* (n.d.). In *King Leopold's Ghost*, Adam Hochschild points out that 'Arabs' in this context were in fact African-Arabs: Swahili-speaking Muslim Africans from territory that is today Kenya and Tanzania – 'Arabs' was a term used to summon up hatred in Europe by the anti-slavery campaigners. For more on the economic history of East Africa, see Jeremy Prestholdt, 'On the Global Repercussions of East African Consumerism', *American Historical Review*, 109, 3 (2004); 755–82, and Thaddeus Sunseri, *Viliman: Labor Migration and Rural Change in Early Colonial Tanzania* (2002). On the non-existence of 'tribes' as Livingstone imagined them, see Mahmood Mamdani, *Citizen and Subject: Contemporary Africa and the Legacy of Late Colonialism* (1996). The phrase 'second encounter' came to me from Vicente L. Rafael, *White Love and other Events in Filipino History* (2000).

On the press and Anglo-American relationships during the American Civil War, I read Brayton Harris, *Blue & Grey in Black & White: Newspapers in the Civil War* (1999); Bernard A. Weisberger, *Reporters for the Union* (1953); *Centennial*

Newspaper Exhibition 1876: A Complete List of American Newspapers (1876); James Parton, 'The New York Herald', *North American Review*, 102 (April 1866): 373–419; Antoinette Burton, 'Who needs the Nation? Interrogating "British" History', *Journal of Historical Sociology*, 10, 3 (September 1997): 227–48; Adrian Cook, *The Alabama Claims: American Politics and Anglo-American Relations 1865–72* (1975); Martin Crawford, *The Anglo-American Crisis of the Mid-Nineteenth Century: The Times and America, 1850–1862* (1987); and R. J. M. Blackett, *Divided Hearts: Britain and the American Civil War* (2000).

Other references in this chapter come from H. M. Stanley, *In Darkest Africa or the Quest Rescue and Retreat of Emin Governor of Equatoria* 2 vols, (1890); Charles Dickens, *Letters*, edited by Madeline House et al., 12 vols (1965–2002); Samuel Smiles, *Self-Help; with Illustrations of Character and Conduct* (1859); Richard Grant White, *The Fall of Man; or, The Loves of the Gorillas, By a Learned Gorilla* (1871); Augusta Fraser, *Livingstone at Newstead* (1913); Dorothy Middleton, 'The Search for the Nile Sources', *Geographical Journal*, v, 138: 2 (June 1972): 209–24 (after a BBC TV series with David Attenborough on this subject in autumn 1971); Blanchard Jerrold and Gustave Doré, *London: A Pilgrimage* (1872); Peter Bailey, 'Champagne Charlie: Performance and Ideology in the Music Hall Swell Song', in *Music Hall: Performance and Style*, edited by J. S. Bratton (1986), pp. 49–69; documents from the Waller Collection at Rhodes House, Oxford; and Joseph Conrad, 'Geography and Some Explorers', *National Geographic*, 45, 3 (March 1924; the essay was originally published in 1923 under the title 'The Romance of Travel').

Periodicals and newspapers I have used are the *New York Herald*, *The Times*, *Punch*, *Illustrated London News*, *Graphic*,

New York Times, Daily Telegraph, Film Renter and *Appleton's Journal*.
Television and film: *Empire: How Britain Made the Modern World*, Programme 3: 'The Mission', Channel 4, January 2003; *Livingstone* (BFI print, 1927 was available from religious promoters till the mid-1940s to be shown in schools and Sunday schools; *Stanley and Livingstone* (Twentieth-Century Fox, 1939; CBS Fox Video); *Mountains of the Moon* (American film, 1990); *Forbidden Territory: Stanley's Search for Livingstone* (TV film, 1997).

3 'FAITHFUL TO THE END'

Reports disagree as to where and for how long Livingstone's coffin was displayed. *The Times* says it was in the Map Room of the RGS, while the *Illustrated London News* and Augusta Fraser both report it as being in the Council Room. A photograph in the RGS archive shows it lying in the Map Room. Tim Jeal says the coffin was on display for two days, the *Illustrated London News* says a week – but as the funeral was on 18 April, it cannot have been longer than a few days. The former RGS buildings at 1 Savile Row have now been converted into an expensive gentlemen's clothing shop. A bitter dispute rumbled on in *The Times* into the early summer between supporters of Susi and Chuma and those who took Cameron's side, until the newspaper announced, 'We cannot allow this ungrateful controversy to continue in our columns' (5 May 1874).

The funeral of Wellington is discussed in Cornelia D. J. Pearsall, 'Burying the Duke: Victorian Mourning and the Funeral of the Duke of Wellington', *Victorian Literature and Culture*, 27, 2 (1999): 365–93, and John Wolffe, *Great Deaths:*

Grieving, Religion and Nationhood in Victorian and Edwardian Britain (2000). On changing mourning rites, Karen Halttunen is interesting in *Confidence Men and Painted Women: A Study of Middle-Class Culture in America, 1830–1870* (1982). See also W. Cotton Oswell, *William Cotton Oswell, Hunter and Explorer* (2 vols, 1900). James Thomas, *Diana's Mourning: A People's History* (2002), serves as a useful reminder that the media can create, as well as report, a myth of a nation in mourning for a public figure. Dorothy Helly's *Livingstone's Legacy* is good on Waller's euphemisation of Livingstone's prose. Reports of the funeral are taken from the *Illustrated London News*, *The Times*, *Lancet*, *Glasgow Herald* and *Saturday Review*. I also consulted the *Proceedings of the Royal Geographical Society*.

AFRICANS IN BRITAIN

The *Illustrated London News* sent war artists to Africa, and engravings such as 'Natives of Ugogo, East Central Africa' shared its pages in the spring of 1874 with engravings of the Livingstone funeral, such as 'Arrival of Dr. Livingstone's Remains'. The *New York Herald* reported that Wolseley accompanied Livingstone's remains back on his way home from Asante campaign. Some useful material is to be found in Audrey A. Fisch, *American Slaves in Victorian England: Abolitionist Politics in Popular Literature and Culture* (2000), and R. J. M. Blackett, *Building an Anti-Slavery Wall: Black Americans in the Atlantic Abolitionist movement, 1830–1860* (1983). 'English Negrophilism' was reprinted in the *Anti-Slavery Standard* on 1 July 1847, from the *New York Express*. I also consulted *Black Victorians/Black Victoriana* edited by Gretchen Holbrook Gerzina (2003); Sarah Meer, 'Competing Representations: Douglass, the Ethiopian Serenaders, and

Ethiopian Exhibition in London' in *Liberating Sojourn: Frederic Douglass & Transatlantic Reform*, edited by Alan J. Rice and Martin Crawford (1999), pp. 141–65; Patrick Brantlinger, 'Victorians and Africans: The Genealogy of the Myth of the Dark Continent', in *Race, Writing, and Difference*, edited by Henry L. Gates (1986); and Andrew Ward, *Dark Midnight When I Rise: The Story of the Jubilee Singers Who Introduced the World to the Music of Black America* (2000). Queen Victoria commissioned a large portrait of the group which still hangs in Fisk University in Nashville, Tennessee. I was very interested by Jan Marsh's exhibition at the Manchester Art Gallery, *Black Victorians* (2005) – the catalogue contains some graphic examples of 'coon jokes'. A special thank-you, too, to Derek Peterson for helping me think through possible motives for the servants' mortuary journey.

Other materials referenced in this chapter are from the Waller Collection at Rhodes House, Oxford: Ms letters; *Livingstone Centenary Celebration Leaflet No. 1* (1913); *Order of Divine Service in Glasgow Cathedral Wednesday 19th March* (1913); and Waller's notebook.

Specifically on Livingstone's servants, the standard works are Donald Simpson, *Dark Companions: The African Contribution to the European Exploration of East Africa* (1975) and Stephen J. Rockel, *Carriers of Culture: Labour on the Road in Nineteenth-Century East Africa* (2006), but see also A. Z. Fraser, *Livingstone and Newstead* (1913). For a detailed account of Wainwright's movements in England, see Bontinck, 'Le Diaire de Jacob Wainwright (4 Mai 1873–18 Fevrier 1874)', in *Africa: Revista trimestrale di studi e documentazione dell'Istituto Italo-Africano* (Rome): 32–3, (Settembre 1978–Dicembre 1978): 399–435, 603–4. See also National Library of Scotland Ms letter from Jacob Wainwright, 23 May 1874 (addressee unknown); 'Jacob Wainwright in Uganda', *Uganda Journal*, 15 (1951); MS letters of Stanley from the Keynes collection; George Catlin, *Notes of Eight Years' Travels and Residence in Europe, with his North American Indian Collection* (2 vols, 1848); Kate Flint, *The Transatlantic Indian* (forthcoming; and Carolyn Steedman, 'Servants and their Relationship to the Unconscious', *Journal of British Studies*, 42 (July 2003): 316–50. I first read about Waller in Twywell in the *Northamptonshire Black History Project News*, 1, 2 (June 2003), and I am very grateful to Jenny Bradshaw for taking me around the church and showing me the relevant editions of the *Twywell Parish Magazine* (1898).

4 STANLEY

Much of the biographical information in this chapter came from the books on Stanley listed under Introduction. Late in the writing process Tim Jeal was kind enough to send me a pre-publication copy of his *Stanley: the Impossible Life of Africa's Greatest Explorer* (2007) which will now become the standard biography. Other references in the section on Stanley and boys are to Stanley, 'Preface', *My Kalulu: Prince, King and Slave: A Story of Central Africa* (1873); Stanley, *Coomassie and Magdala: The Story of two British Campaigns in Africa* (1874); Stanley, 'Anglo-Saxon Responsibilities', *The Outlook* (1899); Ernest Duvergier de Hauranne, *A Frenchman in Lincoln's America* (1974–5); *Last Journals of David Livingstone*, edited by Horace Waller (2 vols, 1874); and Dorothy Tennant, 'The London Ragamuffin', *Illustrated English Magazine* (June 1885): 602–5.

On boys' stories see Hugh Cunningham, 'The Language of Patriotism 1750–1914', *History Workshop Journal*, 12 (1981);

Joseph Bristow, *Empire Boys: Adventures in a Man's World* (1991); Kelly Boyd, *Manliness and the Boys' Story Paper in Britain: A Cultural History 1855–1940* (2003); G. A. Henty, *By Sheer Pluck: A Tale of the Ashanti War* (1884); Heather Streets, *Martial Races: The Military, Race and Masculinity in British Imperial Culture 1857–1914* (2004); and John Tosh, *Man's Place: Masculinity and the Middle-Class Home in Victorian England* (1999).

On Stanley and the Congo, Adam Hochschild's gripping account of the establishment of the 'Congo Free State', *King Leopold's Ghost: A Story of Greed, Terror and Heroism in Colonial Africa* (1998), is essential reading and includes extracts from African accounts of the atrocities discussed here. Kevin Grant's *A Civilised Savagery: Britain and the New Slaveries in Africa, 1884–1926* (2005) was immensely helpful in suggesting a slightly different account of the Congo Reform Campaign. Also invaluable are Thomas Packenham, *The Scramble for Africa, 1876–1912* (1991) and Stig Forster et al, eds, *Europe and Africa: The Berlin Africa Conference 1884–1885 and the Onset of Partition* (1988).

On Stanley's commodification, see Thomas Richards, *The Commodity Culture of Victorian England: Advertising and Spectacle, 1851–1914* (1990) and *The Stanley and African Exhibition Catalogue* (1890). Felix Driver's excellent *Geography Militant* includes a discussion of the court case over the treatment of the exhibited boys. I also used Annie E. Coombes, *Reinventing Africa: Museums, Material Culture and Popular Imagination in Late Victorian and Edwardian England* (1994); and *Christie's London: The Africa Sale including the Henry Morton Stanley Collection*, Tuesday 24 September 2002 (2002).

In 1991 the *Musée Royal de l'Afrique Centrale* mounted an exhibition called *H. M. Stanley, Explorateur au Service du Roi* (Illustrated Catalogue, Volume 15 of *Annales Sciences Historiques*, 1991). See the website at http://www.africamuseum.be/museum/renovation/.

On Conrad, see Joseph Conrad, *Last Essays* (1926); Mary Golanka, 'Mr. Kurtz, I Presume? Livingstone and Stanley as Prototypes of Kurtz and Marlowe', *Studies in the Novel*, 17, 2 (Summer 1985): 194–202; Matthew Rubery, 'Joseph Conrad's "Wild Story of a Journalist"', *English Literary History*, 71 (2004): 751–74. On Stanley and modernism more generally, see Marianna Torgovnick, *Gone Primitive: Savage Intellects, Modern Lives* (1990) and Clare Pettitt, 'H. M. Stanley and the *Fin de Siècle*', Introduction to a Broadview Critical Edition of H. M. Stanley, *In Darkest Africa, or, The Quest, Rescue, and Retreat of Emin, Governor of Equatoria* (forthcoming, 2007).

Periodicals referred to in this chapter are *The Times*, *Boy's Own Paper*, *Illustrated London News*, *New York Sun*, *Overland Monthly* and *Out West Magazine* (1874).

The political cartoons which are discussed at the end of the chapter were all found through the University of Kent Political Cartoons database at: http://library.kent.ac.uk/cartoons/.

LIST OF ILLUSTRATIONS

Title Page: Commemorative stamp issued by independent Burundi in 1973. From Peter J. Westwood, *David Livingstone: his life and works as told through the media of postage stamps and allied material* (Edinburgh,1986)

1. *Alphabetical Adventures of Livingstone in Africa for Boys and Girls* (London, 1941) 3
2. L. Du Garde Peach, *David Livingstone: A Ladybird 'Adventure from History' Book* (1960). Illustrated by John Kenney 7
3. Photograph of Livingstone by Thomas Annan 1864. Carbon print 14
4. Palmer Cox, *That Stanley!* (New York: The Art Printing Establishment, 1878) 17
5. Stanley's meeting with Livingstone, the *Illustrated London News* (10 August 1872) 19
6. Still of Livingstone and African villagers singing from the 1939 American film, *Stanley and Livingstone*. From *Stanley and Livingstone: with 16 plates in colour: 100 illustrations and text based on the Twentieth-Century Fox Film Production* (London: Ward, Lock & Co.,1939) 25
7. 'Livingstone attacked by a Lion' from David Livingstone, *Missionary Travels* (John Murray, London, 1857) 27

8. Wax Livingstone on display in Madame Tussaud's
   wax-work museum in the early twentieth century   62
9. 'Stanley and Livingstone set out on a canoe trip'
   from the French edition of Stanley's *How I Found
   Livingstone*   88
10. Still of the Stanley-Livingstone meeting from the
    1925 silent British film *Livingstone*. From Dean Rapp
    & Charles W. Weber, 'British Film, Empire and
    Society in the Twenties: The 'Livingstone' film, 1923–
    1925' *Historical Journal of Film, Radio and Television* 9:1
    (1989): 3–17   118
11. Still of the Stanley-Livingstone meeting from the
    1939 American film, *Stanley and Livingstone*. From
    *Stanley and Livingstone: with 16 plates in colour: 100
    illustrations and text based on the Twentieth-Century
    Fox Film Production* (London: Ward, Lock & Co.,
    1939)   121
12. 'Carrying the Body to the Coast': a magic lantern
    slide from a series of forty images, *The Life and Works
    of David Livingstone*. London Missionary Society
    (*c.*1900)   128
13. Jacob Wainwright on board the *Malwa* with
    Livingstone's coffin   132
14. Livingstone's funeral in Westminster Abbey, the
    Illustrated London News (25 April 1874)   143
15. Portraits of Chuma and Susi in Western and
    African dress, June 1874   162
16. Photograph of Susi and Chuma with Tom and
    Agnes Livingstone and Horace Waller, taken in the
    grounds of Newstead Abbey in June 1874   164
17. Studio portrait of Stanley with Kalulu, London
    Stereoscopic Company *c.*1872   165

18. A replica of the hut in which Livingstone died,
    built by Susi and Chuma on their visit to Britain   170
19. Photographs of carved pews in Twywell Church in
    Northamptonshire by the author   176
20. Photograph of Stanley   180
21. Frontispiece to D.J. Nicoll, *Stanley's Exploits: or
    Civilising Africa* (Aberdeen 1890)   189
22. Emin Pasha and Stanley jigsaw puzzle (1890). From
    Linda Hannas, *The English jigsaw puzzle, 1760–1890:
    with a descriptive check-list of puzzles in the museums
    of Great Britain and the author's collection*
    (London, 1972)   194
23. Photograph of the Stanley and African Exhibition
    of 1890   196

PICTURE CREDITS

Scottish National Portrait Gallery: 2; . Madame Tussaud's
Museum, London: 8; National Portrait Gallery, London: 12,
17; Simon Keynes: 13, 20, 23; Royal Geographical Society:
15 top left, 15 bottom left, 16, 18; David Livingstone Centre
at Blantyre: 15 top right, 15 bottom right.

While every effort has been made to contact copyright holders of illustrations, the author and publishers would be grateful for information about any illustrations where they have been unable to trace them, and would be glad to make amendments in further editions.

ACKNOWLEDGEMENTS

This book was conceived at a very pleasant lunch with Peter Carson and Mary Beard, both of whom have continued to be remarkably patient and helpful throughout its production.

Simon Keynes was extraordinarily generous not only in lending me a veritable library of precious books and papers on Livingstone and Stanley from the collection of his uncle, Quentin Keynes, but also in early expressing an enormous enthusiasm for the project which made it seem exciting and fun. Simon also gave me a beautiful framed copy of the *Illustrated London News* engraving of the meeting of Stanley and Livingstone, which has hung over my desk and helped me on. For all this, thank you. Fellow Profile author William St Clair kindly gave me three nineteenth-century prints of Stanley and Livingstone from *The Life and Explorations of Dr. Livingstone* by John S. Roberts.

Colleagues at Newnham College Cambridge, the English Faculty, Cambridge, and the Department of English at King's College London were hugely generous in offering ideas and thoughts. Claire Daunton, who was then Administrator of the Cambridge English Faculty, found me a room in the new Faculty building, which was invaluable. My colleagues – Peter Mandler, Jim Secord, Simon Goldhill and Mary Beard – on the Leverhulme Victorian Studies Project, based at Cambridge University, have provided intellectual support of the highest possible calibre. My new colleagues at King's College London have also been wonderful, and it is a constant pleasure to work in such a lively and growing department.

In the States, I have very much enjoyed meeting Bill Sisler of Harvard University Press, and would like to thank him for his invitation to present my work on the book to the employees of Harvard University Press in April 2006. I also gave seminar papers about Stanley and Livingstone to graduates and Faculty at Harvard University and Rutgers State University of New Jersey, and gathered many helpful and generous responses from participants at all these events. In Cambridge I stayed with Leah Price, whose modesty and warmth made this a great pleasure, and in New Jersey I stayed with Kate Flint. Kate has been a constant and unwavering friend, as well as a brilliant mind with which to engage – she generously shared her work on the figure of the Native American in Britain, and our conversations were – as they always have been since I met her in 1993 – hugely helpful in thinking through some of the tougher methodological problems that face us in our work.

Towards the end of writing this book, I discovered that Tim Jeal had gained access to the Brussels archive and was working on a new biography of Stanley. He was immensely generous in allowing me to consult a proof copy and my chapter on Stanley has been much benefited by this.

Two anonymous readers for Harvard University Press gave me generous lists of suggestions and comments for which I was very grateful. Librarians have bent over backwards to help me on this project. First and foremost must be Paul Hudson at the Cambridge University Library, who even offered personally to deliver books to me at home when I was ill, and who cheers me up whenever I encounter him in the library. Another pearl was Pamela Matz at the Widener Reference Library, Harvard University, who went well beyond the call of duty to send me details of Palmer Cox's *That Stanley!*. Others who deserve my particular thanks are Debbie Hodder at Newnham College Library; Sheila Mackenzie at the National Library of Scotland; Sarah Strong, the Archives Officer at the Royal Geographical Society; Carol Reekie and Magda Fletcher at the Cambridge Theological Federation, Wesley House; Susanna Lamb at the Madame Tussaud's Archives, London; Paul Cox at the National Portrait Gallery; Karen Carruthers at the David Livingstone Centre, Blantyre, Scotland; and John Oliver and Kathleen Dickson at the British Film Institute.

Many other people have helped over the two years this book has taken to write and not all their names appear here, but I owe particular and specific debts of gratitude to the following: John Bowen, Melissa Calaresu, Fenella Cannell, Becky Conekin, Jenny Diski, Bernhard Fulda, Heather Glen, Mia Gray, Carola Hicks, Graham Howes, Joanna Lewis, Charles Maccallum, Michele Martin, Sarah Meer, Helen Morales, Rebecca Patterson, Derek Peterson, Jen Pollard, Pierluca Pucci Poppi, Sadiah Qureshi, Amy Richlin, Leigh Shaw-Taylor, Sally Shuttleworth, Sujit Sivasundaram, Gill Sutherland, Adam Tooze, James Williams, Barry Windeatt and Emma Winter.

Felix Driver at Royal Holloway College, whom I did not formerly know, undertook to read the whole manuscript purely out of a sense of scholarly community, which impressed me greatly. I am glad to know him now. Other friends and colleagues have read the whole book prior to publication and made excellent suggestions: Peter Mandler, Kirsten Denker, David Inwald, Charles MacCallum and Derek Peterson. My father, Charles Pettitt, sent a series of enthusiastic emails while he was reading the draft, which meant a lot to me. Needless to say, all errors remain my own.

As a closing gesture as I was finishing the book, I travelled to Twywell Church in Northamptonshire, where Livingstone's servants Susi and Chuma stayed in 1874. I was met with extraordinary kindness and enthusiasm there in the form of the Church Warden, Jenny Bradshaw, who not only showed me all the evidence of Susi and Chuma, but also invited me back to her house for coffee and produced all sorts of interesting documents for me to look at. Some of the information she has put together over her years at Twywell has been supplied by John Peet at the Northamptonshire County Records Office and I thank him too.

Helen Pettitt and James Brown have kept me going. As for my husband, Cristiano, and my daughters, Kitty and Marina, they are my three best reasons to stay alive.

INDEX

A

Abid bin Suliman 74
Abolitionists 21
    Livingstone's funeral
        131–2, 134
    race 142
Aborigines' Protection
    Society 189
Abyssinian Campaign
    (1867–68) 204–5
African-Americans
    138–41
Africans in Britain 137–42,
    146–74
Alabama claims 90–91,
    96–7, 101, 110
*Alphabetical Adventures of
    Livingstone in Africa for
    Boys and Girls* 1–2
American Civil War 8–9, 12,
    43–4
    see also Alabama claims
    British role 90–91
    Livingstone 83–5, 88
    New York Herald 78–9
    newspapers 81–2
    Stanley 203
Amoda 44, 157

Anglo-Saxonism 87–91,
    190–91
Animal Crackers (film 1930)
    16
Anthropological Society 43
Anti-Slavery Society 189,
    197
Appleton's Journal 88–9
Arabs 6–8, 11
Ashanti War, Second (1873–
    74) 137, 184, 186
The Athenaeum 35, 138

B

Baartman, Sara 137
Baden-Powell, Robert, Lord
    53, 181, 186
Bagamoyo, Tanzania 68, 127
Bailey, Robin Wayne 68–9
Baker, Sir Samuel 94, 126
Bakonjo people 64
Bakwain (Kwena) people 25
Balch, Edmund 185
Baloka Plateau 31
Barth, Dr Henry 34
Barttelot, Major Edmund
    192–3
Batoka Plateau 37, 40

Bayeíye people 67
Beeton, Samuel 50
Belgian Congo 174, 181,
    188–92, 199–200, 201,
    205–7
Belgium 206–7
Benjamin, Walter 208
Bennett, James Gordon, Jr 9,
    82–3, 84
  popular view of 15
  reports of Livingstone/
    Stanley meeting 99,
    100–102, 106
  Stanley's return home
    95–6
Bennett, James Gordon, Sr
    79–82, 203–4
'blackface' shows 139–40
Blaikie, Dr William Garden
    55–6, 64–5
Blantyre, Malawi 19
Blantyre, Scotland 19–21,
    56–8
Boer War 199, 201
Bogharib 6
Bonomi, Joseph 54
Booth, William 193
Boston Advertiser 100, 103
Boston Traveller 103–4
Boy's Own Paper 182–3
Brighton, John 116, 134
Brighton and Sussex

Medical Society 111–12
British Association for the
    Advancement of Science
    42–3, 109–11
British Empire 60–61, 182–3,
    185–6
  see also imperialism
Brookes, Peter 209–10
Brooklyn Times 104
Brown, Henry 'Box' 139,
    140
Burnham, Viscount 118–19
Burroughs, Edgar Rice
    208
Burton, Sir Richard 43, 44,
    113, 197
Buxton, Sir Fowell 134

C
Cabora Bassa Rapids 40
Cambridge, lectures 1857
    37–9
Cameron, Lieutenant
    Verney Lovett 125, 129
Cape Town, South Africa
    22–3
Carpenter, W. B. 110
Casement, Roger 190–91,
    201
Catlin, George 169
Chiko 157
Chitambo 52, 124, 127

Chuma, James 44
  in Britain 142, 146–7,
    149–50, 153–4, 160–71,
    174–8
  life as Livingstone's
    servant 156–60, 173
  Livingstone's death 55
  return to Africa 173–4
  return of Livingstone's
    body to Britain 10–11,
    126–8
  Stanley 72, 93
Church Missionary Society
  (CMS) 11, 148–9, 150, 155,
  197
Cimlembwe, John 65
Clemens, Samuel L. (Mark
  Twain) 200–201
CMS see Church Missionary
  Society
Conan Doyle, Arthur
  190–91
Congo, River 187
Conrad, Joseph 35–6, 123,
  207–8
Cook, Harlow 185, 203
Cornhill Magazine 78
Cox, Ian 60
Cox, Palmer 13–16

D
Daily Mirror 62–3

Daily News 112
Daily Telegraph 96, 109, 187
David Livingstone: Heroic
  Missionary, Intrepid
  Explorer and the Black
  Man's Friend (1928) 4
David Livingstone Centre,
  Blantyre 28, 92
David Livingstone
  Memorial Museum,
  Northern Rhodesia
  63–4
Dawson, Lieutenant 149
Dick, William Reid 63
Dickens, Charles 36, 80–81
Dillon, Dr W. E. 129
Disraeli, Benjamin 130,
  134
Douglass, Frederic 84, 138,
  139–40
Dugard, Martin 68

E
'Earthmen' 137–8
East India Company 37
Edinburgh Review 34
Eliot, George 36
Emin Pasha 192–5
Empire (TV series) 117–18
'Ethiopian Serenaders' 139
Ethnological Society 43
Eyre, Governor 45–6

F

Farini *see* Hunt, William
    Leonard
Farjullah 126
Farrar, Carus 55, 126, 149
Ferguson, Niall 117–18
Fergusson, Sir William
    132–3
Festival of Britain (1951)
    60–61
Field, Cyrus W. 48
films 16–17, 58–9, 75, 77,
    117–23
Fisk Jubilee Singers 140–41
*Forbidden Territory: Stanley's
    Search for Livingstone* (US
    TV 1997) 83, 86
Fraser, Alice 150
Fraser, Augusta (née Webb)
    Livingstone's African
        servants 146–7, 149–55,
        166–8, 169, 172
    Livingstone's last letters
        52, 104
    Livingstone's portraits 51
    Stanley 179–81
Fraser, George Macdonald
    204
Frase''s magazine 13
Frere, Sir Bartle 145, 161,
    172
Freud, Sigmund 208

G

Galton, Francis 110
Geographical Magazine 119
Globe 99
Gordimer, Nadine 65
Gordon, General 177
Granville, Lord 97, 104
Graphic 108–9
Gray, Simon 193
Great Britain
    see also British Empire
    Anglo-Saxonism 87–91
    attitude to US 115–16
    black Africans in 137–42,
        146–74
    Livingstone as Roving
        Consul 146
    Missionary Travels 32–6
    news of Livingstone/
        Stanley meeting 9–10,
        11–12, 48–50, 104
    return of Livingstone's
        body to 124–33
    Zambezi Expedition 39
Greeley, Horace 80
Greene, Graham 59

H

*H. M. Stanley, Explorateur
    au Service du Roi* (Belgian
    exhibition 1991) 206
Hamoydah 93

Hancock, Major-General
  Winfield Scott 203
Hardwicke, Sir Cedric 58
Harper & Brothers 83
Harryhausen, Ray 28
Helmore, Holloway 39
Henderson, W. 53
Henson, Jim 17
Henty, George A. 183–4
Heshmy, Selim 95, 185
Hoffman, William 184,
  199
Hotten, John Camden 110
Houghton, Richard
  Monckton Milnes, Lord
  129, 144
Hughes, Thomas 55
Hunt, James 43
Hunt, William Leonard
  (Farini) 141
Huxley-Jones, T. B. 61

I

Ilala, East Africa 10, 124,
  126–7
Illustrated London News
  Alabama claims 97
  'Earthmen' 137–8
  illustration of
    Livingstone/Stanley
    meeting 17, 18, 49, 109
  Jacob Wainwright 150

Livingstone's body
  returned to Britain 126
Livingstone's funeral 143
imperialism 43, 44–8, 133–4,
  136, 144–5, 182–4, 187–92,
  200
India 35, 37, 148–9, 156–7
Indian Mutiny 35, 37
Isenberg, Rev. C. W. 149

J

Jamaica 45–6
Jeal, Tim 63, 179–80,
  187–8
Jerrold, Blanchard 113
Jesuits 67–8

K

Kalulu 51, 103, 109, 137,
  143–4, 163–5, 185
Khoikhoi 44
Kingsolver, Barbara 29
Kinsey, Alfred C 16–17
Kipling, Rudyard 200,
  202
Kirk, John 6, 8, 40, 72, 96,
  143, 197
Kololo people 39–40
Kumasi, Gold Coast 137
Kuruman, South Africa
  23–5
Kwena people 25

L

Lady Nyasa 44, 156
Laing, Arthur 125–6
Leopold II, King of Belgium
174, 181, 188–92, 197,
199–201, 205–7
Leya people 64
Leybourne, George 113
Linyanti 30, 44
Listowel, Judith 63
*Little England's Illustrated
Newspaper* 36–7
Livingstone, Agnes
Civil Pension 130
Livingstone's African
servants 163–4
relationship with
Livingstone 25, 26,
43–4, 92
Stanley 114–15, 186
Livingstone, Anna Mary 30,
130, 170
Livingstone, Dr David
13–70
African servants 156–60
American Civil War 83–4
biographies 54–6, 63
in Britain 1856–58 31–9
in Britain 1964–65 42–4
character 85–7
death 10–11
early life 19–21, 56–8

false reports of death
1866 5–6
in film 16–17, 117–23
first journeys 1840–56
23–31
funeral 11, 51–2, 53–4,
124–5, 130–36, 182
heroism 28–9
Last Journals (1874) 52–3,
54–5, 128–9, 136, 146
marriage 24–7, 29–30, 41–2
mauled by a lion 1844
27–8
medical training 22
meeting with Stanley
2–4, 8–10, 13–18, 48–52
Missionary Travels (1857)
4, 18, 20–23, 27–30, 51,
66–7, 84–5, 129
missionary work 11, 22,
23–4
*A Narrative of an
Expedition to the
Zambesi and its
Tributaries* 43
Nile River 5
return of body to Britain
10–11, 124–33
*Stanley and African
Exhibition* (1890) 197
Livingstone (film 1925) 75,
77, 117–20

Livingstone, Mary (née
    Moffat) 24–7, 29–30, 31,
    41–2
Livingstone, Robert 43–4
Livingstone, Tom 104, 151–
    2, 163–4, 166–7
Livingstone, William
    Oswell 8, 130
Livingstone, Zambia 64
Livingstone Birthplace
    Museum, Blantyre 56–8
Livingstone Memorial,
    Blantyre 119
Livingstone Search & Relief
    Expedition 108, 149
London Missionary Society
    (LMS) 22, 24
    *The Life and Work of David
        Livingstone* 55
    Linyanti mission 39–40
    Livingstone (film 1925)
        117
    Livingstone's missionary
        work 29, 145
    Missionary Travels 32
Lualaba, River 6–8
Luanda 30
Lyttelton, Oliver 61

M
Mabotsa, South Africa 25
MacCunn, Hamish 57

Mackenzie, Bishop 40–41,
    177
MacKenzie, John 20, 65
McLynn, Frank 207
Macnair, James 56, 57, 119
Madame Tussaud's 51, 61–2
Majuara 55
Makololo 75
Malawi 148
Malwa 10–11, 125, 131
Manganga people 40
Manyema, Democratic
    Republic of Congo 6
Markham, Clements R. 130
Mebalwe 28
missionaries
    see also London
        Missionary Society;
        Universities' Mission
        to Central Africa
    African 67–8
    Belgian Congo 191
    Cambridge University
        lecture 1857 37–9
    Jacob Wainwright 154–5
    Linyanti mission 39–40
    Livingstone's funeral 136
    Livingstone's missionary
        work 11, 32
    Shire Highlands 40–41
    South Africa 23
    Universities' Mission 5

Moffat, Mary *see*
Livingstone, Mary
Moffat, Robert 23, 24, 113
Mohammed bin Gharib 74
Mohammed bin Sali 74
Morel, E. D. 190
Mozambique 37
Mugabe, Robert 63
Murray, John 27, 33–4, 66–7,
129, 165–6
Musée Royal de L'Afrique
Centrale, Belgium 207–8
Mutesa 155–6

N
Nasik Asylum 148–9
Nation 78
National Geographic 119
National Portrait Gallery 54
nationalism
African 44–5, 63–5
American 77–8, 99–101
English 182–3
Scottish 57–8
New York Evening Mail 106
New York Herald 2, 78–84
Anglo-Saxonism 89–90, 91
British in Africa 116
British response to the
story 107–9
criticism of Young's
expedition 6

public doubts about truth
of story 104–7
reports of Livingstone/
Stanley meeting 73, 92,
94–102
return of Livingstone's
body to Britain 126
Stanley's career with
9–10, 203–5
Stanley's expedition
across Africa 187
Stanley's reception in
Britain 111–12
New York Standard 99–100
New York Sun 106
New York Times 78–9, 117,
119–20
New York Tribune 78, 80
Ngami, Lake 29, 66–7
Nightingale, Florence 36
Nile, River 5, 10, 11, 44–54,
92
Noe, Lewis 106, 184–5, 203
Nyangwe, Democratic
Republic of Congo 6–8,
93
Nyasa, Lake 42
Nyasaland 148

O
O'Flaherty, Rev. Philip 155
Ormsby-Gore, W. G. 119

Oswell, William Cotton
26–7, 66–7, 93, 135, 136–7
The Outlook 200

P
Palmerston, Lord 37
Parry, Elisabeth 22
Philadelphia Post 76
Philip, Marlene Nourbese
66
Phipson-Wybrants, Captain
T. L. 174
Porter, Maggie 141
Portugal 37, 43
Price, Rev. W. Salter 149,
150–51, 154
Price, Roger 39
Prideaux, Captain W. F. 127
Punch 103, 109, 115

Q
Quarterly Review 45

R
race 45–7
African civility 75–6
black Africans in Britain
137–42
'Dr Livingstone, I
presume' 74–6
New York Herald 82–3
Stanley 113, 187–90, 203

Ransford, Oliver 63
Rawlinson, Sir Henry 107
Rawlinson, Mary 107
Reichardt, Herr 53
Religious Tract Society
182–3
RGS *see* Royal Geographical
Society
Rhodes, Cecil 63–4
Royal Geographical Society
(RGS)
false reports of
Livingstone's death
1866 5–6
gold medal 31, 112
Livingstone as explorer
145–6
Livingstone Search &
Relief Expedition 149
Livingstone's African
servants 150, 161
Livingstone's body
returned to Britain 124,
132
Missionary Travels 34
reports of Livingstone/
Stanley meeting 50,
106, 107, 109
Stanley's reception in
Britain 109–11, 112
statue of Livingstone 61
Russell, Captain 95

Russell, Lord 37

S

Sayd bin Majid 74
Schnitzer, Eduard (Emin
    Pasha) 192–5
Scotland 19–22, 57–8, 133–4
Sechele, Chief 45
Sekeletu, Chief 39
Sekwebu 174–5
Sera, Manua 126–7
Sesame Street (TV series) 17
Seward, Dr G. E. 5
Seymour, Chas B. 32
Shire Highlands 40–42
Shire, River 40
Shupanga 156
slavery
    African-Americans in
        Britain 138–9
    American Civil War 12,
        83–5
    Arabs in East Africa 6–8
    Jacob Wainwright 148–9
    Livingstone 6–8, 21, 113
    Missionary Travels 35
    New York Herald 82–3, 101
    Nyangwe massacre 6–8,
        10
    Stanley 113
    Upper Shire region 40, 42
Smiles, Samuel 36, 86–7

Southampton 130–2
Southworth, Alvan S. 116
Spurgeon, Charles 24
stamps 63, 65
*Stanley and African
    Exhibition* (London 1890)
    195–7
Stanley, Denzil 198
Stanley, Dorothy (née
    Tennant) 197–9, 203
Stanley, Henry Morton
    179–210
    American Civil War 44, 83
    Asante Expedition 137
    Belgian Congo 188–91,
        199–200, 201
    British response to the
        story 107–8, 115–16
    'Dr Livingstone, I
        presume' 2–4, 73, 74–6,
        122–3
    early life 22, 110–11,
        202–5
    equatorial Sudan (1886)
        192–5
    expedition across Africa
        1874–77 187
    in film 58–9, 118–23
    How I Found Livingstone
        (1872) 9, 208
    In Darkest Africa (1890)
        193, 208

journey home 95–6
Kalulu 163–5
Livingstone's African
    servants 149, 155, 174
Livingstone's body
    returned to Britain
    130–31
Livingstone's character
    85–7
Livingstone's funeral 11,
    124, 143
marriage 197–8
meeting with Livingstone
    2–4, 8–10, 13–18, 48–52,
    71–7, 85–93, 96–107
My Kalulu: Prince, King
    and Slave 113, 181, 202
New York Herald 80
political career 199
race 45–7, 187–90, 203
reception in Britain
    108–15
staying with Livingstone
    87–91
Through the Dark
    Continent (1878) 183
Tichborne case 103
Stanley and Livingstone (film
    1939) 24, 58–9, 120–23
Stanley, Lord 5
Stewart, James 41
Sudan 192–5

Susi, Abdullah 44, 156
    in Britain 142, 146–7,
        149–50, 153–4, 160–72,
        174–8
    life as Livingstone's
        servant 156–60, 173
    Livingstone's death 55
    return to Africa 173–4
    return of Livingstone's
        body to Britain 10–11,
        126–8, 129
    Stanley 71–2, 74, 93

T
Tanganyika, Lake 6, 87
Tanzania 2–4
Thomson, Joseph 155, 174
Tichborne case 102–3, 105,
    106
Tidman, Arthur 32
Tillim, Guy 205
The Times
    Livingstone/Stanley
        meeting 104, 107–8
    Livingstone's funeral 11,
        53, 134–5, 143–4
    Stanley's obituary 198,
        203
Universities' Mission 5
Zambezi Expedition
    42
Tracy, Spencer 58, 120–22

Twain, Mark *see* Clemens,
    Samuel L.
Twywell,
    Northamptonshire 175–7

U
Uganda 64
Ujiji, Tanzania 2–4, 6, 8, 11,
    18, 71–4, 85–7
UMCA *see* Universities'
    Mission to Central Africa
United States
    African-Americans in
        Britain 138–41
    Anglo-Saxonism 87–91
    British attitude towards
        115–16
    films 119–23
    Missionary Travels 32–3
    news of Livingstone/
        Stanley meeting 9–10,
        11–12, 48–50, 96–102
    Stars and Stripes 77–9
Universities' Mission to
    Central Africa (UMCA)
    37–9, 117, 168, 174
Universities' Mission
    Society 5, 40–41, 67
Unyanyembe 125, 126, 127

V
Victoria Falls 33–4, 63–4, 68

Victoria, Queen 112, 134,
    138, 141, 154, 182
HMS *Vulture* 127

W
Wainwright, Jacob 125–7
    in Britain 142, 146–56,
        169
    Livingstone's funeral
        137, 143–4
    return of Livingstone's
        body Britain 10–11, 131
Waller, Alice 171
Waller, Horace 43
    Last Journals 52–3, 54–5,
        128–9, 146, 147, 166
    Livingstone's African
        servants 127–8, 146–50,
        160–61, 163–4, 166,
        168–72, 175–7
    Livingstone's fame 10
    Livingstone's tomb 146
    Stanley 114
Wardlaw, Ralph 133
Washington, Treaty of 96–7
Webb family 95, 111, 161
    see also Fraser, Augusta;
        Webb, William
Webb, William 43, 133, 143,
    186, 196–7
Wekotani, John 72, 156,
    158–9

Wellington, Matthew 149
Wells, H. G. 49
Wetherall, M. A. 117–20
White, Richard Grant 94–5
Williams, George
    Washington 190
Wilson, Dr 156
Wolseley, Garnet Joseph 137

X
Xhosa 44–5

Y
Yao people 40, 148, 156
Young, Edward Daniel 5–6,
    33, 75, 83

Young, James 11, 146, 161,
    166–7, 169–70, 173

Z
Zambezi Expedition (1858–
    64) 5, 30, 39–42, 156
Zambia 64, 65
Zanzibar 6, 8, 10, 77–8, 95,
    113, 125
Zimbabwe 63–4
Zouga, river 21
'Zulu Kaffirs' 138
Zulu War (1879) 137, 141

PROFILES IN HISTORY

The *Profiles in History* series will explore iconic events and relationships in history. Each book will start from the historical moment: what happened? But each will focus too on the fascinating and often surprising afterlife of the story concerned.

Profiles in History is under the general editorship of Mary Beard.

Already available
David Horspool: *King Alfred: Burnt Cakes and Other Legends*
James Sharpe: *Remember, Remember: A Cultural History of Guy Fawkes Day*
Ian Patterson: *Guernica and Total War*

Forthcoming:
Greg Woolf: *Et Tu, Brute? A Short History of Political Murder*
Emily Wilson: *The Death of Socrates*
Christopher Prendergast, *The Fourteenth of July*